JOURNEYS TO
THE FAR NORTH

OLAUS J. MURIE

ALASKA
NORTHWEST
BOOKS®

Journeys to the Far North was originally published in 1973 by American West Publishing Company, Palo Alto, California, Library of Congress Card Number 72-87741, ISBN 0-910118-30-2

Library of Congress Cataloging-in-Publication Data
Murie, Olaus Johan, 1889-1963.
   Journeys to the far North / Olaus J. Murie.
      pages cm
   "Originally published in 1973 by American West Publishing Company, Palo Alto, California"—Title page verso.
   Includes index.
   ISBN 978-1-941821-73-2 (paperback)
   ISBN 978-1-941821-85-5 (e-book)
   ISBN 978-1-941821-86-2 (hardbound)
   1. Murie, Olaus Johan, 1889-1963—Travel. 2. Canada, Northern—Description and travel. 3. Alaska—Description and travel. 4. Natural history—Canada, Northern. 5. Natural history—Alaska. 6. Wilderness areas—Canada, Northern. 7. Wilderness areas—Alaska. 8. Indians of North America—Canada, Northern. 9. Indians of North America—Alaska. I. Title.
   F1090.5.M87 2015
   917.1904—dc23
                    2015006569

Design by Vicki Knapton

Published by Alaska Northwest Books®
An imprint of Turner Publishing Company
4507 Charlotte Avenue, Suite 100
Nashville, TN 37209
(615) 255-2665
www.turnerbookstore.com

CONTENTS

Olaus asking the fox for the correct camera setting.

by Victor B. Scheffer

This is the true story of a man who believed that humankind would be saved by learning to love and preserve the wild places of earth, large and small. He was a missionary, though he would have screwed up his face at hearing the word. His religion was wilderness.

In his title for the chapter "Flowers on Ice," Olaus Murie used his own idiom to describe the dualism he sensed in the living world. The flowers above the Arctic permafrost are the beauty and wonder of life, filled with color, fragrance and purity. Simple and undemanding, secret in their parts, they are ephemeral but everlasting. Beneath them, the cold, unresponsive ice represents the limiting factor of life, the physical world that every organism is pressed against in the continuing act of survival. The beauty which only the human animal can grasp and the struggle to survive which all wild animals share—both were the source of Murie's vitality.

I have elected to write about the man rather than the book because you are about to read the book for yourself. Murie's language is deceptively simple. He was not a man to waste words or motion. He saw in his mind what was to be done, and he did it. His clear sense of direction was at times an amazement to his friends and at times an exasperation. On one collecting trip that I shared with Olaus he suggested that we discard the meat of all the birds whose skins we saved for the museum. He did not want anyone to think that in killing a duck or a goose, we were prompted more by our appetites than by our scientific zeal. This, I thought, was integrity carried a bit too far!

One day in Alaska, he writes, he made a bargain with a wolverine. He had shot two mountain sheep for the museum, but the afternoon was fading, and he realized that he would not have time to carry both into camp. He saw tracks of a wolverine—a notorious robber of meat. What to do? "I wanted the skin and skull for a specimen; the wolverine would want some meat to eat. So I partially skinned the animal, pulled the skin over the head, laying bare much of the carcass of pure meat. Then I filled my packsack with the other specimen and went back to camp." At daybreak, he found that his plan had worked. "The wolverine had his feed, the museum had the specimen, and the dogs and I still had a supply of camp food."

I first met Olaus Murie in the summer of 1937, when we lived on the motorship *Brown Bear* and made a wildlife inventory of the Aleutian Islands. I saw him last in the summer of 1958, when we joined Justice William O. Douglas on a three-day hike along the Olympic seacoast of Washington in an effort to save the wild character of a few miles of that beach. He wrote to me on October 16, 1958. "I am sorry to see that so many in high places [of government] look upon the ocean as a place in which to dump things. It is about time we began to look upon the world as a whole unit, an ecological unit for man." He saw, of course, what all naturalists in the great tradition have seen so clearly, that a man cannot separate himself from nature and remain a whole man.

As a man grows in knowledge of nature—or wilderness, if you wish— he also grows in humility. Long ago the word *humility* was related to *humus*, the soil. The truly educated man understands and respects his binding relationship to the soil—to the earth.

Let me quote a few flashes from Murie's book and from memory, to illustrate his lifelong engagement with nature, a relationship in which he was wholly accepting, loving, and confident.

On a snowy trail in Alaska he wrote, "I have seen my lead dog, Snook, sail into a mass of fighting dogs with what appeared to be a smile on his face. . . . I suppose we can say that we [humans] simply share with the dogs the joyous impulse to 'do'."

Again, "This was a hungry country. I learned to eat hawks, owls, sea birds—anything that had meat on it. The Indians up here lived a most rugged life; yet they somehow had a kind view of nature, like the hunters who begged the bear's pardon before shooting it." Later: "Annie boiled some bear feet, wristlets of fur still on them—we didn't mind appearances, and they tasted good." And, "I am convinced that in the evolution of the human spirit something much worse than hunger can happen to a race of people."

On the trail to Rainy Pass, he suffered two sleepless nights with toothache. Using a ptarmigan-feather brush, he painted both sides of the gum with tincture of iodine. "Immediately the pain of this remedy was much greater than the toothache it was to cure. . . . Next morning all pain was gone, and I had no more trouble until I reached Fairbanks and a dentist in the spring."

Indeed, as Olaus once remarked, adversity is good for the soul, and every father should take it upon himself to introduce struggle in the life of his son.

For thirty-one years, from 1914 to 1945, Murie earned a living as a field biologist, mainly in northern Canada and Alaska, first for the Carnegie Museum and last for the United States Fish and Wildlife Service. Earlier, he spent two years as a game warden in Oregon, a job which I doubt that he could have cared for. Offers of higher pay and administrative power left him cold. He wanted only to travel, collect, and see—to tease out the relationships between living things and their environment. He became increasingly interested in origins. How did the alpine saxifrage reach the New World? How could a little band of caribou persist in this or that isolated pass? What are the implications—or carryovers—of wildlife behavior in the behavior of human beings?

So intensively did he feel the colors, shapes, and mysteries of the outdoor world that he had to share them with others. On his first trip to the Canadian Arctic in 1914, when every ounce of weight was a burden, he carried a bulky Graflex camera and sketching materials. He knew the value of a diary, which is to say that he had a sense of history. The beautiful paintings that he left to us are not "art for art's sake," but rather expressions of a sensitive teacher who wanted others to stand on the mountain top and see what his eyes had seen.

"We found something to admire in one another," he wrote of his Indian guides. To the best of my knowledge, he liked everyone. He was puzzled at meanness because, I think, he had a feeling that meanness was a waste of time. His way of approaching strangers (such as the Attu Islanders) resembled his way of approaching animals—slowly and warily, but with childlike trust. I used to think him shy; but later I saw that he was simply waiting for "something to admire."

When I last talked to Olaus, he spoke in distress of the Computer Age, artificiality, and of man's abuse of the wild places of earth. I said, smiling, that he was now an *ecologist* and ought to be happy with his new title. He wrinkled his nose and said "Gee!" In his heart he had not changed. The truths he recognized early and spent a lifetime shaping into words and pictures were still the same old truths. He knew it, and I knew it.

FOREWORD

by Donald O. Murie

My mother, Margaret (Mardy) Murie was invited to attend a ceremony at the White House on January 15, 1998. She was ninety-six years old, confined to a wheelchair and had around-the-clock caretakers at her log house at Moose, Wyoming. I received phone calls from people concerned the trip would be too difficult for her. A blizzard was predicted. I received calls from people encouraging me to approve the trip; if necessary they had a volunteer who would drive her and a caretaker to Idaho Falls to take a flight from there. A movie of her life was being filmed. The producers were already making arrangements with the White House to film the ceremony. It was a measure of the esteem and affection with which she was regarded; some concerned for her well-being, others for the continuation of her remarkable story. Mardy did make the trip. She was wheeled up to President Clinton to receive the Presidential Medal of Freedom for her lifetime of work to preserve wilderness. She had already received about every award the conservation community had to offer. She was almost worshipped by the hundreds who came to see her, to bathe in her glow, to be inspired. Her autobiography, *Two in the Far North*, became the bible of her very large circle of friends.

She was called the matriarch of the American conservation movement. Her life, as seen by the thousands who watch the movie or read the book, was like a fairy tale, from her childhood in frontier Fairbanks to her quiet death in her house in the woods. She achieved much, inspired many, but when asked why she did it she said, "I did it for him."

He was my father, Olaus J. Murie, biologist, naturalist, conservationist, artist, writer, educator, quiet leader who never sought fame or fortune. As a child he roamed the banks of the Red River in Moorhead, Minnesota, when he wasn't working at Bosshart's farm to help his widowed mother. Those woods became his playground, his classroom, and his library. He and his younger brother, Adolph, practiced wood craft and survival techniques they read about in books by Ernest Thompson Seton, and Olaus began to develop his skill at drawing and painting. He carried his skill and his passion for the wild through college and into his adventures across the Arctic world.

When Olaus met Margaret Thomas in Fairbanks he found a fellow nature lover. In their walks through the woods he introduced her to the multitude of various elements, large and small, that together produced the wondrous symphony of a functioning undisturbed ecosystem. He read the daily news found in tracks and markings; there where the trail of rabbit tracks end, two sweeps in the snow on either side show the signature of a swooping owl. He could bring the scenery alive; he had learned the language, and he shared it with Mardy, and later with eager schoolkids as well as adults. All through their lives Mardy and Olaus entertained a constant flow of visitors; scientists, conservationists, writers, artists, who came from every continent and all across the United States. They came to discuss problems, share discoveries, get advice, and be inspired.

When Olaus, at the end of his career with the Fish and Wildlife Service, made a speech to fellow scientists, he shocked them all by talking about spiritual values. He knew his familiar and beloved wilderness was not only a functioning habitat for myriad species, but an essential source of understanding and inspiration for human visitors. He said, "Wilderness is where we learn how the universe works."

Olaus began his life in the natural world around Moorhead, Minnesota; he began his exploration of true wilderness in the Arctic and furthered his understanding of how it works, becoming a pioneer of the emerging science of ecology. He helped build a strong scientific foundation to guide conservation policies and efforts. He shared it all with Mardy, who used it in her own style after his death. Her fame has often overshadowed his. I know she would agree that this book should be reissued so more people could make his acquaintance. It's an adventure, a good read, and an insight into the man who moved the conservation world. *Two in the Far North* is Mardy's story; *Journeys to the Far North* is Olaus's story.

This page intentionally left blank

by Margaret E. Murie

Olaus had hardly been sick or indisposed a day in his life when suddenly, at the age of sixty-four, he found himself facing a long hospitalization—more than a year, as it turned out. During the latter months, after he was past the critical period, he began to fill his days by reliving mentally his whole full, active life. One evening when I walked into his hospital room, he lay propped up on pillows smiling at me: "I've been up in Labrador all afternoon!"

That is how Olaus came to write this book. He early made an outline of the chapters and what he wanted the book to hold, but the chapters were not written in sequence. I think he did write about Hudson Bay first, but after that, he selected subjects in whatever order they came alive in his mind.

I know that Olaus felt much of his northern adventure had not been told in his many scientific reports. Though he referred to his early notes as he wrote, he often remarked that too many years had gone by before he had begun to put into his diaries his own feelings about the far places he visited. And it was his feelings about them and their people that he hoped to transmit in his book. I know he believed that one must feel about them before one can realize how vulnerable they are—how much in need of man's protection as a necessary nourishment for his culture.

I am sure it was this strong, though perhaps wordless impulse that kept Olaus writing, a chapter now, a chapter then, during all the busy last nine years of his time here. Those years following his homecoming from the hospital were rich ones and full. Looking back now, I am amazed at all he accomplished. He was still director of The Wilderness Society, so there were many speaking engagements and hearings on wilderness matters; the Wilderness Bill was being agitated through Congress; the amount of mail we handled at our home in Moose, Wyoming, sometimes seemed unmanageable; and we went on two all-summer expeditions to the Brooks Range of Alaska. (As I recall, the chapter called "Flowers on Ice" was written in his notebook while he sat on a mossy bank above the Sheenjek River.) During these same years we were both working when we could on our joint-authorship venture, *Wapiti Wilderness*, which Olaus also illustrated. From time to time he would do illustrations for books by other authors as well.

In winter we could give attention to all of these things, except when we had to go off to some conference or hearing. But summer was a different tale, for then the world came to Jackson Hole and quite a bit of it to our door. Besides, the charms of the valley and the Tetons were constantly calling, "Come out! Come out!" Streams, lakes, forests, river bottoms, mountain slopes, and canyon trails were all to be savored again every summer.

But Olaus was one who used every moment, and his book continued to take shape. He seemed able to close off his surroundings and concentrate whenever a thought struck. I have memories of his sitting at a table under the back windows of the big living room at Moose, writing away while four, five, or seven children, grandchildren, and guests were conversing, playing cards, arguing over a crossword puzzle or a game of Scrabble. He could have gone into his study and closed the doors, but he seemed to find harmony and warmth in the midst of the people he loved.

Often Olaus would join in the conversation, and often it was about the Arctic—the chapter he was writing or the picture he was drawing. I remember particularly a lively argument about protective coloration. So in a subtle but real way, all the people who were close to Olaus have had a part in this book.

When Olaus was fourteen, his teacher Miss King called him aside as he was marching out with the other eighth-graders of Moorhead, Minnesota, on the last day of school. At first he thought he had done something wrong, but she said, "Olaus, I want you to promise me something—keep on drawing!" In those later years, when he was illustrating his own and others' books both in pen and ink and in color, we wished that he could have found Miss King to thank her. Aside from that drawing class in grade school, he never had an art lesson. He just "kept on drawing." Even before he was out of college, Olaus always carried drawing paper in the back of his field notebook and found things to sketch at every spare moment. By the time he began to think of a book about the Arctic, he had a wealth of sketches in the files to remind and inspire him.

I hope the readers of this book will enjoy traveling north with Olaus the scientist, the observer, the artist—above all, with Olaus the lover of nature and of his fellow men. To me, this book is more than anything an adventure narrative that portrays an era in the history of the Arctic, both Canadian and Alaskan, that is now gone and cannot be recaptured, an era that holds an authentic and worthy place in our history. I don't think Olaus meant this to be any serious scientific treatise. He simply had an overwhelming desire to share with others his experience of the North. It was an experience difficult to repeat now, but I know that he cherished the hope that the young might still have opportunities for great adventure if only our society is wise enough to keep some of the great country in both Canada and Alaska empty of development and full of life.

This page intentionally left blank

PART I

EXPERIENCES IN THE ARCTIC

This page intentionally left blank

HUDSON BAY AND LABRADOR

Up to Great Whale River

The great opportunity came not long after my graduation from Pacific University, while I was working for the Oregon state naturalist William Finley. An expedition was going into the Far North—country where there were still blank spaces on the map. My friend Stanley Jewett had been asked to go but could not, and this gave me the opportunity to apply for his position as assistant.

In 1914 many of us young people were reading avidly about exploration in little-known regions and looking to the north for adventure. We often heard of the "jumping-off place," where you left behind established means of living and went off to explore unknown country. I began packing my gear in Oregon with this exciting phrase running through my mind.

On this occasion Carnegie Museum of Pittsburgh was sending another expedition to Hudson Bay under the leadership of the veteran ornithologist W. E. Clyde Todd. I was to be his assistant and collect museum specimens—I, only a novice in preparing specimens, although I had practiced it informally for several years. Here was my chance to go north, to see, to learn, to find out!

Late in May we arrived in Cochrane, Ontario, the end of train travel and the other mechanics of civilization. There we met our two Ojibway

Indian guides, Paul Commanda and Jack. When I saw them walking taciturn and expressionless in the village of Cochrane, the white man's domain, they did not seem impressive. Were these two to take us to the Far North?

After a few days we made our start. We and our equipment were taken out to the bank of the Bell River, where the eighteen-foot Peterborough freight canoe was waiting. Here in their own domain, the Indians came alive. Paul, the chief guide, slim and athletic, took charge of the loading. Jack (whom we somehow called "Jocko"), tall and capable, was equally efficient.

I looked around. We were on the bank of a river thickly flanked by spruce forest as far as one could see. This was our "jumping-off place!" Before us, stretching far into the north, lay the unknown.

The canoe loaded, we got in—Paul in the bow, Jocko in the stern, and Mr. Todd and I in the center. All we two had to do was paddle; the Indians would guide the canoe.

From now through all the summer months, the canoe would be our home, along with the simple camp we would make each night. As I look back now to that memorable first trip, I tend to ignore the scientific data we gathered, the specimens we collected, important as these were. There lingers much more clearly the remembrance of those many days of canoe travel— the lakes we crossed, the rivers we went down, the water, the rapids, the inviting shorelines. Added to this was the thrill of noting and collecting birds along the way. Each night I also put out mouse traps, and altogether we made a collection of data and skins that would add to the fund of such knowledge in the museum. But aside from the necessary work for which expeditions are sent out, there are impressions one gets which seem aimless at the time but which add much to the personal value of a remembered journey.

I remember I found out something about myself that first day—a surprise to me. I had thought I was an expert with the canoe. That was at least one thing I could feel familiar with, for I had had years of experience on the Red River in Minnesota. We boys had even built our own canoe, using barrel hoops for ribs, with a covering of sturdy wheat sacks, which were in common use at that time. But here on the Bell River I soon saw something different. We had a long way to travel, and our Indian guides were really going places. Their paddle strokes were quick and powerful, and we all had to keep the fast rhythm set by Paul in the bow. How different from the lazy Sunday-afternoon kind of canoeing! Nothing was said. The Indians set the pace, and in time we got used to it. This was canoe travel in wilderness. The canoe was an Indian invention and these Indians knew how to use it.

As we slid rapidly down that river, I kept looking at the forest along the banks. What was it like in there? We had glimpses of birds, little ones, like certain flycatchers and sparrows which live in the north woods, and larger ones like the ravens. As we camped, I explored back from the river and collected specimens. That was my job, and I was eager to make good on this my first expedition. I remember when I brought in the first specimen, a ruffed grouse; how embarrassed I was as Mr. Todd watched me skin the bird! After all, he had only my word that I could do these things. On the other hand, he won my admiration when I noticed that he could identify every little sound a bird made. Certainly his notes were eminently authentic. Once in a while, whenever I had a few spare moments, I would make a sketch of a bird, in black and white or in color. Today these sketches mean a great deal to me.

We traveled along, got acquainted, found something to admire in one another. We were all different. I became very interested in the Indians, their skills and their characters. And they taught me much about canoe travel. The endless stream of water going down the river channel in varied country is not always placid. There are rough places filled with boulders and, downhill, the river rapids. All this was new to me.

When we approached and looked down on the watery turmoil ahead, I thought: "Are we going down through that in the canoe?"

Yes, we were. There was some conversation in Ojibway between the two guides, evidently over planning the route. Then down we went. I was grateful that the Indians were in charge. I just sat there paddling hard when they told me to and trembling with fear as our big canoe bounced around like a feather among the rocks, where water was pouring over, whitened by the speed and turmoil; we would bounce off a swell, meet another one, and ride over. Right away I learned to do what the Indians told me. We had to reach a speed greater than the rushing water in order to go where we wanted; otherwise we would drift onto the rocks, smash over, and the river would have its way with us. So, contrary to my instinct to hold my breath and hope for the best as a rocky lump in the water rushed toward us, I would paddle hard for *greater* speed, and we would glide by at one side. Time seems long in an emergency, but we were going fast, and it must have been a very short time before we would glide into a quiet pool below the rapids. It was over, and we were still afloat!

Our route was not all river travel. Sometimes we portaged across to a lake or another stream. I was glad the Indians knew where we were going and how to get there. All I had to do was paddle, carry a load over the portages, collect specimens on shore, write notes in my diary about birds seen along the way, and enjoy the passing Canadian scene.

In the diary I find the following notation for June 8:

"In the evening olive-backed thrushes, water thrushes, and a white-throated sparrow were singing, nighthawks were swooping, and an occasional chirp of some other bird was heard, making a pleasing combination with the twilight."

What a varied life—adventuring on river and lake, seeking scientific knowledge, and enjoying beauty!

The lakes also taught me something, for I had always canoed on rivers. On the large lakes, where winds had the say of things when they came, we found it necessary to calculate carefully before starting across. Sometimes we had to stay in camp a whole day while the wind whipped up big whitecaps. Sometimes we would start traveling as late as four o'clock in the afternoon, whenever the weather would let us. But these periods ashore gave me an opportunity to explore the woods, prepare museum specimens, and sometimes make another drawing.

Those woods! In there were down logs, bushes and many kinds of plants, birds, signs of rodents—all that goes with a coniferous forest environment. Here was a forest exhibiting the true balance of nature's process.

Aside from the aesthetic quality of such a place, it had great scientific value in the emerging phases of ecology.

We had not been many days on our trip when I became aware that this northern wilderness was populated. This, I found, was canoe and Indian country. All travel in summer was by canoe, and the travelers were Indians and a few fur traders, with occasional inquisitive scientific parties like our own.

This was brought home to me vividly one evening. We had made our camp on the shore of a big lake. All was quiet, and dusk was approaching when I heard a rhythmic sound. I looked out in the direction it came from, and there appeared a long canoe with at least seven Indians crossing the lake. Their paddles all dipped in unison, and all the bodies leaned forward with each stroke, the sounds coming across the still water with strong, repeated emphasis. There, in the twilight on a smooth lake, was a beautiful symbol of Indian life in this north country, with the canoe and its inventor in one appropriate setting.

A few days later we arrived at a Revillon Frères trading post on the shore of another lake, with an Indian camp as part of it. The post surprised me, but I was to learn that these adventurous fur traders had gone into many far places in the north. We stopped there to camp.

After a while I paddled out on the lake with our empty canoe to photograph the shore. I had given little attention to an offshore wind until I wanted to return to camp. Then I was in trouble. The canoe bow rose high in the air; sitting in the stern, with the wind swinging it one way and then another, I found I had a real problem. Just then I noticed a row of Indian women standing on the shore watching this inexperienced white man trying to make the canoe do what he wanted it to. This scene did not help my morale. I was sure the stern of a canoe was the proper place from which to steer it. Struggling desperately, I finally managed to make long slants with the wind on the quarter and eventually reached shore. Paul waited there to help me beach the canoe. He used one of the nicknames he and Jocko had given me as he said quietly: "Baptiste, next time just get in the bow, kneel down, and paddle right in to shore."

Each day was different. One day I wrote in my journal: "Painted a violet." Another time: "Sketched a nighthawk."

We found nests of ravens. One day's notation: "Camped on Sugar Loaf portage. An Indian camp there—two women, three children, and some dogs. The men were off after supplies."

One day we were going down through the tumbling waters and big waves of another rapids. We were having a lot of experience with white water, and I was getting used to it, but I was still apprehensive each time we went into it. We were paddling hard in this one, and I watched each wave closely as it approached us. Then I heard Jocko's quiet but urgent voice behind me:

"Baptiste! Give me your paddle!"

Without looking I reached my paddle back and felt his hand take it. I just sat there, watching the white water around us. Soon we were safe in the quiet water below, and we all relaxed. The others had been so intent on the canoe problem before us that they had not heard Jocko's request. Now we learned that halfway down his paddle had broken in two—and he in the important position in the canoe! I was glad I had passed my paddle very quickly in response to his quiet request.

One day Paul surprised me. I don't remember exactly what our conversation was—possibly I was making a confession to him, with whom I had become pretty chummy, but I remember not wanting the others to know how scared I was in rapids. Paul made the statement, "I never go through a rapids without being scared. I know just how little it takes!" Paul, of all people—our chief guide, who made his living running rapids! I have often remembered his words, especially when, years later, I was climbing a high mountain in the Rockies with an experienced climber and guide, who admitted his fear when he negotiated narrow ledges with a sheer drop of hundreds of feet. At any rate, my own fear of the rapids seemed more reasonable after Paul's remark.

We had been about a month on the way when, on June 26, we reached Rupert House, a prominent Hudson Bay fur trading post on James Bay. We were through the forested canoe country and had reached salt water. Now new plans had to be made. There were Indians at this post, some white people, dogs, buildings—something different in this great expanse of wild country. But here, too, while others were preparing for our further trip, I kept busy collecting specimens. I found pet birds and a pet fox living with the Indians, and many sled dogs. Truly we had reached the north country.

I find in my notes for July 2:

"In the muskeg I heard a fine, long-drawn, 'squeaky' *cheep* and followed it up. When I finally found the bird, it proved to be a hermit thrush. In the evening I went out again and found one singing in the top of a spruce—one of the finest songs I have heard. Everything else was still, with only the muskeg all around and the softening glow of the sunset. The bird itself stood out boldly against the sky, as if it intended to have an audience."

Little beautiful things—big plans—but here was human living in the wilderness. Before us, to the north, was Hudson Bay country.

At Rupert House we had to make new plans. Our chief guide, Paul, with whom I had become very friendly, was not feeling well. He had a chance to go to Charlton Island, in James Bay, where there was a small community with a doctor. We hated to have Paul leave us but agreed that he ought to go. To take his place, we obtained the services of William Morrison, who had been a guide in Labrador and was experienced. On the advice of local people, we also obtained a larger canoe, twenty-one feet long.

In the few days at Rupert House I saw a way of life all new to me. The Cree Indians lived here in colorful tipis; I could not resist making a watercolor sketch of one, with an Indian woman entering it. There were sled dogs, including some small ones said to be the original type of "Indian dogs." I never had a chance to investigate this further, but I did see an Indian family that had a captive fox. It aroused a kindred feeling, for once as a boy in Minnesota I had kept a fox in a cage. Did these Indians have the habit of keeping pets? I wondered.

On the day of departure—July 3—we set out in our twenty-one-foot seagoing canoe. This was different. Gone was the intimacy of rivers and lakes, and even the rapids which I had enjoyed being frightened in. Now, stretching out before us to the far horizon in the north, was salt water, the biggest "lake" we had yet ventured out upon. What would it be like up there?

The weather treated us well, but we had our share of rolling waves to contend with. Occasionally, when we had a fair wind, we put up a sail. A sail on a canoe! That was also new to me—another instance of my inexperience. In the evening we went ashore to camp. That, at least, was familiar routine, and a woodsy environment that was homelike. Each night found us camped at the edge of the forest, after a day on the open sea.

In a few days we reached East Main, another Hudson Bay trading post up the coast. We stayed over for a day there, while Mr. Todd and I identified birds and put up specimens. There was always a crowd of Indians watching us stuff the small birds. What would the white men think of next! But here, for some reason, the Indian girls were very shy. One group I met fled back to their village. Were they afraid of me? A number of us were gathered one day in one of the houses where there happened to be several Indian girls. They crowded into a corner like frightened wild creatures and would not even look up. Was I beginning to learn about the Cree Indians?

Again we packed into our canoe and continued on up the coast. My journal says little about this day—July 10—but it has become a spectacular day in my Hudson Bay memories. The day had seemed long and monotonous. We were continually paddling against a head wind and fighting moderate waves, one after another, hour after hour. Willie, who must have known where to go, told us we were far from the usual route of travel. But he thought this was the best way, and the rest of us relied on his judgment.

Eventually we saw ahead of us a small island. When we reached the lee of this little bit of land, we decided to go ashore to rest a bit, for we were tired from our long battle with the waves. As always, we took the paddles with us when we stepped out, and I took with me the skinning outfit, including a coil of wire.

It took me only a few minutes to explore this little treeless bit of land, as we all scattered to stretch our legs. I saw one pair of willow ptarmigan, but there was not much else. To make use of the spare time ashore, Mr. Todd and I settled down to prepare some specimens. There were always some waiting to be taken care of, and we had to make use of all the time when we were not traveling.

A little later, as we sat there busy with the specimens, I happened to look up. "Look there!" I exclaimed.

There went our canoe, drifting serenely away! For a moment I was fascinated by that widening gap of water. Then suddenly the thought struck me—it was I who must act, for I was the only swimmer in the party.

I jumped up and called the guides, who came rushing up, shouting in their own tongue. Once I was on the move, the brief moment of consternation was gone. I felt relieved, almost joyous, for that should not be much of a swim. I quickly took off my clothes. As I see it now, I may have made a mistake there. Short as the delay was, by the time I trotted down to the water's edge the canoe had drifted considerably and was moving at an alarming rate.

I plunged into the water—and received an icy shock which left me gasping for breath. I quickly reached swimming depth, still struggling for breath. Little waves dashed water in my face, and in my unsettled state I was unable to keep from swallowing gulp after gulp of bitter salt water. In a few moments the first cold shock had passed; I regained my breath and attended strictly to the business of swimming.

By this time the canoe was far enough out to catch the full sweep of the wind against the mast and furled sail, and was making good progress. Already it seemed far away. I pushed on with all my strength—I simply had to catch that canoe!

How long did I swim? I don't know. One does not think of time in an emergency. I was working hard, but I could see that the canoe was gaining.

Then something else was happening. I began to feel a numbing sensation at the small of my back, seeming to reach inward to quench the source of all my activity. I must hurry even more, for I realized then that our lives were at stake—and certainly my own life was precious to me. But a deadly chill was creeping over me as I floundered in the icy water. The power had gone from my strokes, and a sense of disaster crept into my heart. Cold and low in spirit, I struggled on, stupidly wondering why the canoe grew small and indistinct. When I felt a cramp in one leg, I knew I had lost the race; and as I looked back at the island, now far away also, a panic came over me. Land, any piece of land, seemed so good. I headed back for the island. Could I make it?

I can't remember much about that return swim—I moved more and more slowly. But one does not give up easily when life is immediately at stake—and I am here now telling about it! I do remember finally touching bottom and stumbling up the beach. I was so numb I could hardly feel the gravel under my feet. Mr. Todd was there reaching for me and helped me over to a lively fire he had built. How gratefully I leaned over and practically embraced those flames!

I was so concerned with my own immediate needs that I was unaware of what was going on. But when I was a little warmed and still alive, I looked out toward the canoe. Out in the water I saw another craft, and Mr. Todd explained to me:

When Willie and Jocko had seen that I was losing the race, they found a few small drift logs and lashed them together with my coil of wire to make a crude, makeshift raft. They climbed aboard, fore and aft, took their paddles, and began the long, slow journey. When I looked, standing naked beside the warm fire, they were already small in the distance. Then Mr. Todd and I saw something else. Far out there was another small island whose windward beach would stop the drift of the fugitive canoe. The two Indians paddled on. It was no longer a race—they only had to reach the stranded canoe. When they boarded it with paddles, all was under control once more.

It is interesting, at a time of more leisure, to appraise such an experience. At one moment all seemed against us—we must fail. But I did get back to the island alive. More important, we had taken paddles with us ashore, there happened to be a few driftwood logs on the beach, I had taken ashore a coil of wire, and above all, our guides had seen the possibilities and used their ingenuity to save our lives. All these details had worked to effect our rescue. How can one understand such things?

For several days that little island was home, this time with the canoe well up on the beach. I was in bed, recovering from all the seawater I had swallowed, until on the second day Mr. Todd brought me a big cup of cocoa. That settled my system, and next day we continued our journey northward, once more taking note of bird life and looking forward to normal adventures.

How different things can be! A few days later we camped on a rocky shore, and I see in my diary that at this camp I was painting flowers. That evening I wrote:

"The sun was setting behind the island as we landed; the little dark, stunted trees were outlined against the colored sky. A flock of ducks flew by and with the gleam of the rich light on the water made a beautiful picture. As we came ashore, a robin was singing—a welcome sound up here. We also heard some white-crowned sparrows."

We were now traveling in what ornithologists call the Hudsonian Life Zone, next below what they have named the Arctic Zone. At this place we found bear skulls hung in the trees by Indians, but I did not learn the full story about this until later. Also, in these waters I saw my first white whale— an animal I was to know better as time went on.

On July 22 we reached Fort George, another Hudson's Bay Company trading post. Again we had the hospitality of the place and another glimpse of human life in such a wilderness outpost. Two days later, on Sunday, the missionary Reverend Walton held services. We all went to church, where were assembled all the Indians and white people of the village.

Here at Fort George we also heard of a tragedy. At Cape Jones an Eskimo with two boys had been out from shore, presumably in a kayak, when a heavy squall struck, and they disappeared.

We ourselves had to round Cape Jones, and a few days later we reached the scene of the tragedy. Here is another occasion vivid in memory. There was a northerly wind, and as we came up in the lee of the cape the water was smooth. We moved along easily, but out beyond the point we could see white water.

"Pretty rough water out there," Jocko warned from the stern. No one made any decision to stop here to camp. Jocko didn't feel that he was boss, and only made that mild suggestion. But when we got around the point, we realized what Jocko had meant. We really were in for it!

We were suddenly confronted by huge sea rollers. We couldn't turn; we had to go ahead and hope to make it to a bay farther on. Each wave as it came on us was a problem. I earnestly hoped our guides had the skill to cope with it. I glanced over to the land, and there on the skyline of Cape Jones stood a row of Eskimos, no doubt watching to see if we would make it. It didn't make me feel a bit better. Up high, then down low in the trough, then up again. How long could we keep this up? I was scared, but I kept on with my methodical paddling. Mr. Todd and I had nothing to do with managing the canoe. Then a human voice broke into my thoughts. It was Jocko, in the stern behind me.

"Pretty big swell, hey *Shogenosh*?" I heard him chuckle. When we kidded each other, he always called me *Shogenosh* ("white man") and I called him *Ishinabe* ("Indian"). Apparently he saw how scared the head of the expedition was, but how could he chuckle at a time like this? This was serious, no question about it—but I felt better. I imbibed some of the confidence of my friend in the stern. And after a struggle which seemed hours long but was actually less than an hour, we reached the haven of the little bay we had seen in the distance and, with enormous relief, made camp for the night.

So it went—observing and collecting birds, writing our notes, plunging into situations where our lives were in danger, and at other times seeing only the beauty around us. We are not always the same, are we? The night before this emergency, encamped on an island, I had enthusiastically recorded in my diary:

"There was a beautiful aurora tonight, extending across the sky overhead from horizon to horizon. It made a lovely scene as I watched the glow of the tents in the distance, the wide stretch of the barren island, and the aurora overhead."

There was something vital to the purpose of the expedition about Cape Jones. No matter in what direction we go over the globe, we find something different. Natural forces are constantly at work on our planet, shaping the character of different parts of it. One of the most fascinating aspects of our life experience is to try to understand these natural influences. We had just succeeded in getting around this cape, and when Mr. Todd and I had time to look around, we were both impressed by what we saw.

In the first place this high ground was treeless. Wandering over it, I saw an arctic hare in the distance; up to now we had seen only snowshoe rabbits in vast wooded areas. To the north of us we could see forests in the distance along the main line of the coast. We knew the arctic hare would not be found there. But here on this cape were a few birds and plants which were characteristic of the Far North. And here were Eskimos in their favorite environment of open country, living off the sea. In short, Cape Jones, jutting out into the sea between James and Hudson Bays, was a little piece of the true Arctic. Here was a piece of land reaching far enough into the sea to be influenced by oceanic climate and far enough north to display a little bit of true Arctic environment. Later I was to learn that islands farther out to sea—yet far south of Cape Jones—are also treeless and have an Arctic character. Such is the influence of the oceanic climate on islands far south of the normal limit of trees.

On a trip such as ours there are days and days of busy work. It was not a pleasure trip, but we had pleasures—frequent, unexpected, interspersed with the routine work.

We worked up the coast of true Hudson Bay, north of Cape Jones. A strong wind at our back sent us up the coast at a rapid rate. On the afternoon of August 6, we arrived at Great Whale River, the goal which had been set for that summer's expedition. The whole Indian population stood on the bank watching our approach. As we stepped ashore we shook hands with every one of them. We were given a warm welcome by the trader, Mr. Maver, and were soon comfortably encamped.

There were the typical few buildings of a Hudson's Bay Company trading post, including the small dwellings of the permanent assistants at the post. Here we were to stay until the little steamer *Inenew* arrived to take us south to Moose Factory. Our northward canoe trip was over. At Moose Factory we would begin another 180 miles of canoe travel upstream to Cochrane, Ontario—and then home!

But we spent some days exploring the backcountry at Great Whale River, coming on lakes, bluffs, and the varied fauna in each setting. And we got acquainted with the Indians. The *Inenew* finally arrived on August 24. The unloading was interesting to watch. Every Indian pitched in, carrying flour bags, boxes, and kegs. Little boys tugged and tussled with bags, or two of them together would roll little kegs up the walk. And so the ship was unloaded.

At this point in my story I should mention something about myself. At that age, only a couple of years out of college, I thought I knew everything. I found myself arguing with Mr. Todd about little, unimportant matters. He carried in his hind pocket a huge telescope. When he saw an interesting bird, he would reach back for the telescope in order to identify the bird properly. Each time I would tell him what the bird was before he could bring his telescope to bear, and I would feel very superior!

One day we saw a bird in the distance on a beach. "Greater yellowlegs," I announced—but then wished I could retract my words.

"Hudsonian godwit!" he exclaimed excitedly when he got the telescope focused. This was a rare bird for us.

Mr. Todd made no reference to my mistaken identification, but he made me feel a little better when he suggested that I go get the bird, which I did.

At another time we were on a small island. Mr. Todd found a brood of ducks, shot the female, and wounded one of the downy young. Holding the wriggling youngster in his hand, he called across to me, "Won't you come here and kill this wounded bird? I don't have the heart to do it."

I hurried over, squeezed the sides of the body over the heart, and it died immediately. Then I burst out: "You were willing to let those other ducklings go without a parent, but you are unwilling to kill this wounded duckling in a humane way!"

As usual, I was unaware of certain human attitudes—that it is sometimes hard for a person to appear cruel to himself in order to perform a humane act. But on the whole, Mr. Todd and I got on very well, and I am sure all members of the party really got much pleasure out of the trip.

We had a hard time getting south on the *Inenew*. We started out against some big swells and had not gone far when I began to feel sick. As the boat pitched and rolled more and more violently, I became seasick in earnest. There were three little husky pups on the deck. One began wailing piteously, trying to keep its feet on the deck; its mouth frothed, it hung its head, and looked very miserable indeed. I sympathized with that pup—I was not the only sick one. Soon our guide Willie succumbed, then husky Bill's son. I gave up, went below, and found a bunk. When I awoke, it was quiet; we were back at Great Whale River—too rough!

We waited for a day of much better weather to start southward again. Stopping along the way at various places, it took us several days to reach Charlton Island. There we learned that there was a war in Europe!

A Winter in Eskimo Land

All summer we had traveled together—down rivers, across lakes, up the east coast of James Bay into Hudson Bay—taking notes on animal life and collecting specimens for Carnegie Museum. Now we were back down at Moose Factory, at the southernmost part of James Bay. Here we went out on the tide flats where blue geese and other waterbirds congregate for a month each fall before continuing their migration south. Paul Commanda, well now, had again joined our party. One hundred eighty miles of upriver canoe travel separated us from the "jumping-off place" at Cochrane.

The north had appealed to me—its freedom and its beauty. I had given much thought to it. I didn't have definite plans but I just wanted to be there. I wanted more.

Finally I talked to Mr. Todd: "Couldn't I be up here another year? I am sure I could add to your ornithological information by studying the winter life here."

Mr. Todd was sympathetic. He wanted scientific winter notes from this country and winter specimens for the museum. But he said, "I am sorry; I don't have the authority to keep you on salary."

He went as far as he could. "The only thing I can say is that I am sure we of the museum can help you sell any specimens you are able to get up here, and I can arrange a letter of credit with the Hudson's Bay Company at Montreal, in the amount of your summer's salary. [I think I was getting one hundred dollars per month, or slightly more.] But you will have to be on your own."

I was elated by his cooperation and made arrangements to stay in the house of Mr. and Mrs. Moore, employees of the company, there at Moose Factory.

Next morning I said good-bye to my summer's companions and stood on the bank, watching them paddle up the broad Moose River toward civilization. I turned to face a year of a far different way of life—to spend a winter in this far country.

Not all travelers had yet left the country. Robert Flaherty and a companion had been up on Baffin Island, where Flaherty had been getting material for his famous film *Nanook of the North*. I was thrilled by his account of experiences up there. I wanted to get farther north too!

One day at Moose Factory I came up to him as he sat on the porch of the store. In the course of our talk he shook his head and exclaimed, "I would like to go over there and strike that Kaiser!" and I could understand. The war had begun, and all legitimate or high-minded civilian aspirations were secondary.

In a little while only permanent residents remained at my new home, Moose Factory (now called Moosonee). This village, the center of the Hudson's Bay Company fur trade for the whole Hudson Bay area, occupies an island near the mouth of Moose River. A long line of buildings extended down the shore of the island—an imposing array in comparison with the small cluster of houses I found at the more northern trading posts. There was a big store where goods were traded to the Indians, the residence of the district manager, a church and parsonage, various storehouses, and a number of small dwellings. These were the homes of the Hudson's Bay Company "servants," as they were called, and a few Indian families. At certain seasons the place would be enlivened with Indian tipis along the edge of the woods bordering the little hay meadow behind the post. Enough hay was raised here to feed a few head of stock and enough potatoes to supply this post and some others farther north.

Across the river was the post of the rival "French Company," Revillon Frères. In the following weeks I learned that the Hudson's Bay Company people referred to the other as "The Opposition," and the Indians called them *Opsheeshun.*

I soon got acquainted with the Moores, my hosts for the winter, and felt lucky. They were friendly, honest, considerate folk.

It was still autumn, October, and while everyone felt that winter was imminent, we still had some good weather. On October 20 I witnessed an important preparation for winter. On this day they hauled up on the bank the little *Inenew* (meaning "Indian") steamer that visited the various fur trading posts, and on which we had come down from Great Whale River. To do this they used every bit of strength in the village, human and animal. In front of one of the buildings was a capstan with a great heavy cable reaching down to the ship. Skids had been laid on the beach for the ship to slide on.

When all was ready everyone—Scotchmen, Indians, a horse, and an ox, pushed and hauled on the spokes of the capstan, round and round, until the boat was safely lodged in its winter berth above the water.

After this important job they all celebrated with whiskey (except the horse and the ox). I find in my journal for the next day the comment: "They were a sadder-looking lot when they went to work this morning."

My life that winter was varied. I became better acquainted with the Cree Indians. Many of them came to visit the Moores, with whom they seemed to have friendly relations. But one day an Indian woman came to vent her wrath on Mrs. Moore. It seemed that kindly Mrs. Moore had given an Indian boy some meat to eat. Here was that boy's mother, greatly perturbed. Among the Indians, an animal was always divided into "woman's meat" and "man's meat." Mrs. Moore had unknowingly given the boy woman's meat.

"Now, dat boy have sore back when he get big!"

This was only one of the many superstitions the Cree Indians had. Several times an Indian would bring Mr. Moore a beaver to eat. Later the Indian would return to get the bones, which he tied in a bundle and hung above the ground in a willow.

Then I learned about their behavior toward the bear. If an Indian came upon a bear while hunting, he would first make a little speech, which I cannot give verbatim, but which was essentially an apology to the bear for the necessary killing. When the bear was killed, its body was carried in on a blanket. The cleaned skull was decorated with black and red bands painted across the forehead and hung in a tree. Such were the bear skulls I had noted along the east coast during the summer. One white man in the village smiled at this custom of making a speech before shooting a bear. But does not this represent a stage in human appreciation of our associated environment, which has widespread expression as Albert Schweitzer's thought of "reverence for life"?

These Indians appealed to me in many ways. One evening a group of us went out to a flat island to hunt ducks. We left our canoes at the shore and went far inland on our hunt. It was dark when we turned back, but we stumbled along, following a couple of Indians who were leading. Presently one of the other white men turned to me and asked, "Where do you think our canoes are?"

The land was flat; we could only see dimly a little way around us. I pointed in a direction that seemed right to me, but I didn't really know. The Indians chuckled, and we trudged along in silence. Then suddenly, there were the canoes! How did those Indians know?

While writing this account of experiences with Indians in the Hudson Bay country back in 1914, I am interested now, in 1962, by the necessity of examining critically some bills currently in Congress aimed at laying waste some of the beauty of our outdoors—with huge appropriations for the purpose. And I wonder: can we compare the hectic, unethical motivation in our vast effort to change the face of the earth, with the simple, honest motivation shown by those Indians facing coexistence with fellow creatures in their environment? Which is the more worthy, from the standpoint of human, spiritual progress—those of us who blindly use machinery and kill polar bears in the Arctic from airplanes, or those who many years ago felt humbly apologetic in shooting down a bear? We can smile at primitive beliefs, but it is the human motivation behind them that counts.

As the season went on at Moose Factory I collected specimens, for I had the zeal to add to our scientific knowledge and to add specimens to the museum collections somewhere. But, also I could not help being aware of the culture I was living in. There were, of course, the alcoholic sprees found anywhere. Here they occurred on special occasions, to celebrate something. On the other hand, my blacksmith-landlord, Mr. Moore, often sat reading the Bible of an evening.

There were other activities. During the whole snow-free autumn the snow buntings and especially the horned larks were about in flocks. Two boys with whom I often associated would hunt them with bow and arrow. One of the boys was the Moores' son Harry; I don't recall the name of the other. Most of the white people here, the "servants" of the Company as they were called, were Scottish. I used the American way of pronouncing words, and so pronounced Harry's name in this soft manner. One day the other boy undertook to correct me: "Not Harry—*Hah-rry!*" And he rolled the *r* delightfully.

I have always had a strong feeling for color, whether in the sky or in the earthy landscape. It was still autumn weather on October 30, when I wrote in my notes an account of what I saw at Moose Factory, apart from anything human:

"This evening was perfect. The water was smooth, reflecting the dull, deep gold of the nearer islands, the deep blues of the more distant spruce woods, and in the west one little daub of coppery red gleaming through the dark trees where the sun had gone down. The clouds were tinted a dull purplish, deepening in the eastern sky. Along the shores is a narrow edging of ice, drifted upriver by the tide, tinted a delicate purplish pink with blue shadows. It was a rare, peaceful scene, a fine northern autumn evening, which makes one glad to be alive and makes indoor work seem unbearable."

Two days later, on November 1, I looked out to see snow falling quietly, whitening everything. Later in the day it grew colder and blew hard from the northeast, drifting the snow. The trees were whitened by the moist snow, and the river looked dark in contrast. A few snow buntings went whirling by among the snowflakes.

The significance of all this came to me that evening. Just before dark I heard excited voices outside. When I hurried out, I heard someone call, "The wavies are going!"

At first there was only a babel of voices in the darkening snowfall, but soon I made out dim lines of birds flying by in the distance. They were the "wavies," the blue geese, and a few white ones, all going up the river, flock after flock. Winter had come to this southern outpost of Hudson Bay, and the birds knew it was time to leave.

In the spring and summer these geese had nested on Baffin Island and in other parts of the Arctic north of Hudson Bay; they had come down to spend a month in the autumn on the lush tidal flats of James Bay. Now their delightful feeding vacation was over and, in response to long racial experience, they set off in the first real snowstorm on the next long journey to the southland, near the Gulf of Mexico. They knew! The next day more flocks were passing over.

A strange feeling came over me as I listened to those bird voices. My companions and others had gone by canoe back to civilization, the horned lark flocks had gone, and now the geese were leaving. Winter had come to the northland, and I was entering a new life experience. But in spite of these thoughts, I was looking forward to it. What would a Hudson Bay winter be like?

When the last flock of geese had gone, we felt indeed that winter was with us. Only a few kinds of birds now remained—the chickadees and redpolls, the warmly feathered owls, and some other hardy northerners. The ice on the river gained in volume and strength until it reached clear across. And it snowed until the landscape shone in purest white.

But I was not the only newcomer staying on in the north. Among the buildings were some English sparrows, virile explorers who, I was told, had first come to Moose Factory about five years before to make it their home. The sparrows occasionally met disaster, as we all do. One day I found one hung by the neck in a fork of a tree, the work of the shrike or "butcher bird" who hangs up such carcasses until it needs them for food.

This brings up something about the language of the Cree Indians. The gray or Canada jay they called *wiska-zhon-shish*. It means, as it was explained to me, "the little one that works at a fire," referring to the fact that these jays come intimately to a campfire for any food they can find. Undoubtedly, here is where we got our name "whiskey jack" for this friendly bird. My friend Mr. Moore, the blacksmith, the Indians called wiskazhon, because he worked at a forge. He was a big burly man, so they left off the final diminutive syllable *shish*.

As for the shrike, the bird that had hung up the sparrow, they called him *weethigo wiskazhonshish*—the "bad spirit Canada jay." Of course, when we translate from one language to another we can only approximate.

Wiska-zhon-shish! As usual the Indian name is most appropriate, for normally in the north whiskey jacks are at hand when a campfire is built, looking for scraps of food. No sooner does the thin smoke of a campfire begin to rise than the feathered visitors appear. Little gray shadows float into the limbs of the trees about you, and hopping from branch to branch, the silent birds draw as near as they dare. They eye you cautiously and cock their heads at the fire, carefully sizing up the situation. Just show your hospitality by tossing them a few crumbs, and how confiding they become!

To the lone traveler the whiskey jack (or gray jay, as he is now called) is a companion. He comes to share the fire built for the noonday or evening meal and brings a sense of fellowship, a bit of life in the silent forest. Familiar and companionable as he is, he is also a bird of mystery. He can easily remain invisible among the trees when he wants to, especially in the nesting season. He does not wait for warm spring weather but builds his nest in

March, while the snow is still deep. So quiet and secretive is he at this season that the nest is very difficult to locate.

FAR NORTH, AMONG PEOPLE AND A CULTURE STRANGE TO ME—HERE WAS A way of life I had only read about, and I was in it! One cannot enumerate all the activities of such a winter, but some things stand out which have meant much to me in the years since. I learned that a stream valley nearby, called Maidman Creek, had no Indian trappers claiming it, so I took that as my hunting and trapping ground for museum specimens.

I can't remember how my hosts adjusted to my way of doing things. In the first place, they thought I should have a thermos of hot coffee in my pack when I was away all day up Maidman Creek. "No thanks," I assured them. "All I need is a sandwich for lunch. When I get thirsty I just chop a hole in the ice." They couldn't understand that but saw that I meant it.

There are memories of Maidman Creek! One day I watched three otters having a fine time. One after another they coasted down a high, snowy bank, sliding on their bellies. At the bottom was an opening in the ice, so they slid right into the water at the foot of the slide. They came up through another hole, clambered out on the ice and up the bank for another slide. Over and over they did this, seemingly in pure joy.

On other days I found otter tracks in the snow showing places where they had taken a great forward leap, sliding a few feet on the snow. Surely they were having a playful, happy life here in the snow country.

One night I was sitting on a bank in the moonlight. I heard a slight, mysterious tapping sound in the snow behind me. I sat still, but very slowly turned my head, just in time to see a weasel coming hippety-hop to investigate me. The weasel is curious and vigorous in its movements. This one came right up to me, nosing about to see and to understand about me before he pattered off over the snow, disappearing in the woods like a dim moonlight shadow.

Once I came upon an open space in the creek. There must have been a warm spring there to keep this bit of water from freezing. A small group of mallard ducks apparently knew this pool would remain open and were taking a chance on spending the winter there. In later years in Alaska I found similar open places, some even north of the Arctic Circle, occupied by ducks and by water ouzels. This little sprite, the ouzel, or dipper, takes advantage of such open places in the snowy winter and exhibits the virility of its little life by *singing* through the winter!

These were some of the glimpses of life on Maidman Creek. There were other things, too—such as a literary adventure that did not require snowshoes or lunch. One Sunday I remained in my room most of the day reading *The Silent Places* by Stewart Edward White. What a treat it was to see how such a sensitive person could tell about living in just this kind of country—a varied country, with streams, forests, tamarack swamps—"the silent places."

Then came Christmas! At home in Minnesota we had always had a Christmas tree and all the usual domestic trimmings that go with that day. What would it be like up here?

About the middle of December a "packet" came up from Cochrane, eight days by dogteam. In the mail were letters from home, a Christmas box, and the book *The Man Without a Country*. Here was I, too, in a far country. It was especially warming to get word from home, the first in a long time.

Christmas is celebrated variously in different countries, many of the activities being the result of tradition. Here at Moose Factory the Indians took advantage of some of the white man's tradition. It was the custom for some of them to bring a stocking or a little bag to the houses to be hung up, and on Christmas day they would come calling for them, hopefully.

The highlight of the day for me was being invited to attend Christmas dinner in the evening at the home of Mr. Wilson, the head of the Hudson's Bay Company for all of Hudson Bay. I felt a little strange among these very British folk because of their speech and their way of doing things, but it was a wonderful meal. At dessert time came another tradition I had only read about. Through a door of the living room where we were assembled came Mr. Wilson's daughter, carrying a plum pudding aflame with brandy, the ceremonious climax of our Christmas dinner.

As I became better acquainted and entered into the life of this little community, I gained an impression which was strengthened by later experience. There was an atmosphere of the remote past. Oxen were still used to haul wood. There was an apparent lack of hurry in all activities, as if the powerful trading company, with a tradition and history dating back to 1670, need not join in the modern rush of the business world. Perhaps rush and hurry were not necessary in dealing with the northern Indians and Eskimos.

There were other things that had also come down in history—the long Indian history before any white men had come. The Hudson's Bay Company initials were sometimes interpreted as "Here Before Christ." It is true they had been there a long time; but the Indians had been there long before that, and the white people at Moose Factory had I learned some of the unwritten Indian history and mythology. One day Mr. Moore told me an Indian "yarn," as he called it. Some Great Spirit—I don't know what he was called—portioned out to the animals the fat they were to have on their bodies. One by one they were dipped in a lake of grease. The rabbit got anxious and jumped into the lake before his turn came. The Great Spirit was displeased with this selfish action, so to punish the rabbit he took him up and pulled him through his hand, wiping off the grease. For his disobedience the rabbit was to go without his share. But between the shoulders, in the little cavity back of the neck, a small portion was left after he was wiped off. To this day that is the only place where the rabbit has any fat.

Truly, the Indian is a close observer; and like all of us, he has tried his best to interpret observed facts. What shall we think of our attitudes and feelings about the world about us? Beauty is present in all parts of the world, but my being in what was then considered the Far North may have conditioned some of my reactions. In my diary for December 27 I find the following, written for myself:

"Sunday. I read all morning and in the afternoon went across to the "French Company" to a gathering to sing. I enjoyed it more than the church service here, for there was such an evident feeling of sincerity. As I was coming back with Willie Moore (the Moores' older son), the moon came out, and I saw it was going to be a rare night. It has been mild today with snow falling most of the time.

"After tea I put on my warm cap and deerskin mittens, and went out for a walk. I believe I enjoyed some of the best moments of my life. I went along the 'Northwest Path.' The trees stood around me—masses of spruce, a rich, soft black, the spire tops outlined against the bright, moonlit sky and here and there silvered over with a coating of snow. As I walked, I looked through openings or lanes among the trees, where the soft but clear moon-shadows stretched across, and rounded snow mounds and snow-covered logs were outlined by their delicate shadows. On the level snow and over the snow sprinkled trees sparkled the 'diamonds,' and over all, high in the sky, shone a clear moon. I walked along the path, here gazing up at the wonderful moonlit trees, there looking in among the trunks into a little opening flooded with light, or along a lane where the delicate shadows mingled wonderfully. Small bushes seemed frosted over and sparkled. Everything seemed crystalline, yet strangely mellow. There was a feeling of purity about the whole thing, as if I were in a holy place—so much so that when I heard someone shout to his dogs in the distance it felt painful, like a discordant note in music.

"I finally came to the river bank out at the back of the island, and here was another scene. The wide, smooth expanse of the river was bounded by the distant, dark shores of the islands. I crossed over to Charles Island and wandered about on a diminutive lake, and finally turned back as a thin, cloudy haze began to dim the shadows and obscure the wonderful purity of the moonlight. In such surroundings a man feels elated, no task seems too big, and all evil thoughts disappear."

One day in late January I went through some swamps to "Mi Lord's Ridge." I was crossing one of these snowy "plains," head down against a wind, when I became aware that grouse were running around me, in all directions. These proved to be a flock of about eighteen sharp-tailed grouse, feeding among the scattered dwarf birches and paying little heed to me. The birds would run quickly, then stop abruptly at a little bush, picking away vigorously at the seeds or buds for a moment, only to scurry off to another bush. From time to time one or two of the hindmost would fly along and alight near the front of the band. They appeared very busy, although at times one or two would crouch awhile in the snow, possibly because of my presence. They all carried their tails straight up, and there was a low conversational "whistling" as they fed.

In such snow-covered "muskegs" I found a border of tamaracks, the small deciduous cone-bearing tree common to these places. Years later I found a few sharp-tailed grouse living in a limited tamarack woods in Interior Alaska. Apparently the muskeg-tamarack environment is an agreeable home for the sharptail in the north country.

On the way back on this January day, as I plodded along on snowshoes, I came on the place where these grouse had spent the night under the snow. Each one had tucked itself away underneath, and the snow which had fallen that night and drifted had covered it nicely. In the morning they all had simply pushed up and out and begun feeding. This made me recall boyhood days in Minnesota, when very often prairie chickens would burst out of the snow at my feet when disturbed by my approach to their snug retreat. Willie Moore told me that the sharp-tailed and spruce grouse do not sleep under the snow in springtime when crusts form. But the ruffed grouse continues to do so, and some get frozen in by a strong crust. These birds have learned, as many outdoor people have, that in the cold of midwinter it is warmer under the snow blanket.

So many things to learn about during this first winter in the north! I knew, of course, that the snowshoe rabbit has a more or less regular "population cycle," a building up of numbers for ten or eleven years to a "high," followed by a "crash" in numbers. In the winter of 1914–15, these rabbits were at a high, then as the season went on they began to die. There were rabbits everywhere. I got all I wanted in a snare line. At one of the stores frozen rabbits were piled up like cordwood. I bought a rabbit-skin sleeping bag from an Indian for fifteen dollars. The skins had each been cut spirally in a long narrow strip and then woven—one hundred and eighty skins in that one blanket. I made a sleeping bag out of it and used it in various parts of the north for many years.

I was told that when a dogteam made a trip anywhere that winter, the dogs were easily fed by the dead rabbits found along the way.

Stories of dogteam trips were working on my imagination. I had vaguely planned to go on north sometime, but now my plans began to take shape. I decided I must leave the friendly people of Moose Factory and go northward—whenever the opportunity came along.

IN THE LATE AFTERNOON OF JANUARY 27, A BITTERLY COLD DAY, I WAS working on some specimens in my room when I heard a shout outside: "The Rupert House dogs have come!"

I hurried out. There in front of the store was the mail packet, a team of ten dogs. The dogs lay resting on the snow, and beside the sled stood the driver, the same Willie Morrison who had been our guide in our summer canoe travel. Willie was trembling with cold, and black patches on his frost-bitten face suggested what he had been through. He was waiting for his partner Charlie Hester to find out where they were to put the dogs. When Charlie came out of the store, they quickly unharnessed the dogs and tied them to the palings of a nearby fence. Someone from the store brought out a bundle of frozen rabbits and chopped them apart with an axe. At the sight of food the dogs leaped to their feet, tugging at their chains and howling in chorus. They kept it up until the men had tossed a couple of chunks to each dog. They seized the frozen carcasses and gulped them down in an unbelievably short time—then looked for more. But when they realized that no more was coming, they calmly curled up to sleep in the snow. The sun was setting by now; it was growing dark.

I had run out thinly clad and was feeling the bite of the cold. The sight of Willie shivering there and the dogs' frozen repast sent a chill through me, and I was glad to run back into Mrs. Moore's warm kitchen. My enthusiasm for a dogsled trip north cooled.

But plans had been made, and on the morning of January 30, when the mail team was ready to go back to Rupert House, 100 miles east, I was ready, too. This would be my first experience with dog-sledding. As we were saying good-bye, with a group assembled beside the flat fourteen-foot sled, I realized more keenly than ever what my stay with the kindly people at Moose Factory had meant to me. It was like leaving home again. Mrs. Moore had carefully wrapped a cake for my birthday in March. To the last minute she was looking out for my welfare, even braiding a pair of garters for my moleskin leggings while the dogs were being harnessed!

With a shout from Willie and a shove to loosen the runners, we were off on the long trail. The familiar landscape of Moose Factory drew away; the line of buildings grew smaller. We passed island after island where I had hunted—Pilgrim, Middleborough, and finally Ship Sands. The river widened; the north shore became a faint blue line in the distance. Then we were fairly out on "the coast," where the white expanse of James Bay spread to the horizon. Here the storm-driven snow was packed hard and the pulling was easier for the dogs. We went through Cabbage Willows and past Blackberry Point; then one of the landmarks of this region, Sherrick's Mount, loomed up blue and white in the winter landscape.

We trotted along beside the loaded sled, the two guides in front to steady the load in rough places. Occasionally one of us would hop on for a ride to rest a bit, but not for long. The sled was heavily loaded, and furthermore we had to run to keep warm.

That first day runs in my memory as a pleasant dream. The novelty of this new kind of travel was fascinating. We pitched the tent that night at the edge of the woods, ate a hearty meal of fried moose meat, biscuits and tea, and rolled into our rabbit-skin blankets—what greater comfort could one wish?

Now, in retrospect, I want to be back again, with a loaded sled creaking its way over rough ice or running smoothly and quietly over level places, with a good team of dogs trotting steadily in front, muzzles low, tails waving high—and the snow stretching away until broken by the blue line of woods where we might camp for the night.

I never tired of watching the husky dogs at work. Hitherto I had only seen them loafing about camps in summer, filthy, mangy-looking beasts, kicked and beaten at every turn. They certainly seemed like unpromising creatures. As winter came they improved in appearance, but I had never seen them at work until this trip. Just as I had admired the Indians in their performance in the rapids, so now I admired the huskies. It is well to withhold judgment of anyone until you have seen him at his best. These dogs—well-furred, tireless, efficient—were at their best in harness, on the winter trail.

As we traveled on, each day seemed colder than the last. There was always a wind. Finally, as we struggled along, wild thoughts would shoot through my mind: "Can we keep this up long enough? Will that flimsy tent be protection enough against this furious weather?"

We had no thermometer, but I learned later that on at least one night it had been forty degrees below zero. The guides complained very little, yet they were not dressed as warmly as I, who had a couple of layers of warm woolen clothing topped by a parka and leggings of Hudson Bay moleskin cloth. Charlie, the silent one, had an ordinary winter coat and a small scarf around his throat. His face was bare to the wind, but he didn't get a single frostbite. Willie, who wore a hood over his head Eskimo style, was frequently frostbitten, further disfiguring his misshapen face. But he also seemed indifferent to it all. In all my days with Willie, I could not see that he was ever moved either by pleasure or pain.

It was a great sight when, on the fourth day, we made out the snow-covered roofs of Rupert House in the distance. In a little while the guides began to adjust their caps and clothing, and to check that the load was all lashed in neatly. The arrival of the mail packet was an important event at these northern posts, and the guides were preparing for their dashing entry into the village. The dogs understood, too, and increased their speed until we could hardly keep up with the sled. With a dash we started up the bank below the store—and the sled tipped over. "Hell!" was the silent one's comment as we all hurried to right the heavy sled.

The hospitality shown me at this trading post, the comfortable evening meal with Mr. Nicholson the trader in his warm living quarter—only someone who has had a similar experience can imagine these pleasures. But the visit here was brief. The dogteam from East Main had been there for several days awaiting the mail from the south and would start back in the morning. The guides agreed to let me go along, and I was eager to get as far north as I could.

Next morning we were again speeding over the sea ice, the two Indians from East Main and I. In such open-surface sledding the dogteam is harnessed to the sled in a far different way than in wooded country. Each dog had a towline tied to a central point on the sled. Each line was of a different length, the leader having the longest one, so he could be out in front. The whole arrangement was fan-shaped, so the dogs with the shortest traces were far out to the sides. From time to time some of the dogs would change position, crossing from one side to the other, passing under or over the other traces. Thus the traces would become tangled, forming a sort of braid next to the sled which little by little worked forward. Twice on this day we tried to stop the team to undo this tangle, but the dogs were wild to keep moving, so we let them go. This team was by far the liveliest of my whole trip.

My knowledge of Cree was very limited, and the two Indians knew very little English. I wanted to get acquainted, so I tried to ask one of the drivers what he called the porcupine in his language. Mustering what little Cree I knew and using signs, I said: "*Peyuk mistik—mitsu, mitsu, mitsu*" ("One tree—eat, eat, eat"). I was trying to tell him that this animal often spends days in one tree, eating the inner bark. The driver knew porcupine habits so well that he broke into a big smile, told me the Indian name, gave me to understand that there were some porcupines back in the forest. At least we had communicated!

East Main is only seventy miles from Rupert House, and we arrived on the second day. Now I had a long wait, for no dogteam was going north for many days. But I had a profitable and restful time in the quarters of the friendly trader, Mr. Jobson. He had been in the service for about forty years, and I learned from him a good deal about the life of the Indians. I was surprised to learn of several cases of cannibalism among them. In a few instances, when a family was starving back in the "bush," one member—generally the husband—had attempted to kill some of the others to allay his own hunger. In most cases, some or all escaped from the cannibal and eventually reached the nearest trading post, nearly dead with fatigue and starvation. Then I remembered a comment Mr. Wilson of Moose Factory had made as he pointed out a passing Indian: "He had a snack off his wife last winter."

These cases are rare, but hunger is not rare, particularly farther north. The Cree Indians were primarily hunters and had not learned to hoard or lay up for the future. This was not so much the fault of the Indian as of circumstances. The Crees depended on hunting, directly or indirectly, for both food and clothing. The depleted game supply of the Labrador Peninsula is a variable quantity, unreliable and deceiving. The food that the Indian bought at the trading post, with the winter's fur catch, was often used up before the next winter's trapping began.

One of the most astonishing natural history notes I got from Mr. Jobson was his account of the passenger pigeon, now gone forever. He said "wild pigeons" had been common in the 1860s. He saw them on Albany River, Moose River, and one at Woswanapi as late as 1884. His description certainly fit the passenger pigeon: bluish, with a reddish breast, long tail, and "small feet." They flew about in flocks and fed on berries. Mr. Jobson had even seen them in burned woods; sometimes they alighted on houses.

It was not until February 17 that I could press northward again. Then there were several teams going toward Fort George.

One night in an Indian camp stands out in my memories of this part of my journey north. Running through a spruce forest, we came to a large wigwam. I could see that it was made of upright poles set close together and apparently covered with moss, but the details of its architecture were not clear since it was coated with snow. It seemed very large for a wigwam, but still I did not guess there were as many Indians living in it as we saw when we stepped inside. In the center were two roaring stoves. Around the edge, bordering the wall, ten families found room to spread their blankets and stack their belongings, each family appropriating a certain space. A place was cleared for my sleeping bag, and my grub box was carried in and put beside it.

I had wondered about the Crees, with their ill-fitting "civilized" store clothes, in this wilderness environment. But this camp was something different, some of it dating far back in their history. The floor of the wigwam was covered thickly with spruce tips, wonderfully smooth and level. Most of the men were away somewhere, but the women were busy. At one side of the door a young woman was industriously weaving a rabbit-skin blanket. With slender brown fingers she deftly handled the furry white strips. Another woman was cleaning fish. Several others, in a group by themselves, were busy picking cones off spruce boughs and dropping them into a kettle. I wondered what kind of brew that was to be. Above them hung an arctic fox, recently trapped. It was a picturesque bit of Indian household activity.

After a little warming by one of the stoves I went outside to look around. A small group of children, dressed in rabbit-skin clothes, were coasting down a little slope on a small toboggan. Like children farther south, these youngsters enjoyed a frolic in the snow, but they were also unconsciously training themselves for the work of grownups. In his winter travels in the forest, the Indian uses a small, slender toboggan such as these children were using. Now several more women came into camp, each hauling a log through the snow for firewood. A good supply had been cut and piled neatly in front of the wigwam. A little later the men came in, one by one. I gathered that they had been tending their fish nets, set under the ice.

Here was the winter home of the Indians. I appreciated their hospitality, but it was a restless night. Children cried and complained continuously. Some were evidently sickly, others just hungry. During the evening I had from time to time given a biscuit to some complaining youngster until, before I realized it, my supply was very low.

At other camps, too, I heard the hungry crying of children, and I kept giving away my food. The birthday cake went, and I ended up eating dog food. My Indian companion on this part of the trip was surprised that a white man would do this; and I, in my ignorance, was surprised that he was surprised. What was the custom of this northern country?

My visit at this camp impressed on me more than ever the uncertainties of the Indian's life. He was never many meals ahead and depended largely on hunting, in a land where game is never plentiful.

After several days' travel on the coastal sea ice, my Indian companion and I arrived at Fort George, another typical Hudson's Bay Company village and post, several buildings at the edge of the coastal forest.

That evening in the house of the trader, where several white people of the post had gathered, I had an embarrassing moment. I had spent so much time with Indians in these past weeks that I had begun to speak like them.

The Crees on the Labrador side of James Bay had a very vigorous way of speaking. Their word for "yes" is *eh-heh*, pronounced quickly and vigorously. When I meant to say yes to a question that evening at Fort George, I heard myself saying, "*eh-heh*"—not at all the smooth "uh-huh" of a white man.

Here at Fort George I heard another story of cannibalism. In the store an Indian woman was pointed out to me. "She and her husband were camped back there in the woods," the trader told me, "and they ran out of food. As they were starving, she sensed that her husband was planning to eat her. So she somehow escaped from the camp and made it in to this post." I wondered what happened to the husband.

My visit at Fort George was very brief. Mr. Maver, the trader from Great Whale River, was there and was returning north the next morning. I was invited to go with him.

After we had said our good-byes in the crisp wintry air, the team started off. As I ran forward to keep up with the sled, I stumbled and fell flat in the snow. I remember the trader's laughing voice calling after me as I picked myself up, "That's a bad start you made, young man!"

This lap of the journey took five days of dog travel, with Mr. Maver, his Eskimo dog driver, and his fine team. (No white man ever drove dog-teams in this part of the world.) I soon realized how fortunate I was to be traveling with Mr. Maver, who was friendly, outgoing, and helpful. I knew that he was liked by everyone on the entire coast and that he was very able. He held the key post of the region, one aspired to by all beginners in the service of the Hudson's Bay Company.

Most of the time we all three trotted beside the sled—riding was too cold. But I knew that when the chief factor made an inspection trip of trading posts up the coast, he lay on the sled all the way, wrapped in many blankets and robes.

We spent one night with an Eskimo family in their tent. The atmosphere in that family group was cheerful and warm, although I later learned that for two days they had been without food—no seals.

I learned another thing on this coastal trip. The Eskimos, who had lived here for numerous generations, had observed and come to understand the physical factors affecting winter travel. As usual the undersides of the sled runners were covered with steel bands. But for the colder part of winter the Eskimos had improved on this. They applied a warm, wet mixture of mud to the bottom of the runner over the steel, shaping it like a round, mud tire. The mud quickly froze solid in the extreme cold. After smoothing the surface, they applied warm water, which quickly froze into a perfectly smooth coating of ice. Runners so treated slid smoothly over the winter landscape. I was told that at Moose Factory they sometimes used soft cattle manure instead of mud.

When the ice coating wore down, the driver would heat some water and apply a wet coating over the surface again with a rag. This froze at once, and we again had a glass-smooth runner to glide over the snow.

Before we reached Great Whale River there came a day when our driver tipped the sled over on its side and knocked off all the mud. "He must feel that the colder part of the winter is over," said Mr. Maver. "From now on there will be some thawing, and for this the steel runners are better."

A little after noon on February 27, we saw ahead of us a group of snow-covered buildings. In the bright blaze of February sunshine, the world appeared white and dazzling—the season of dusk and dark was over for that year, and we were arriving at Great Whale River! Slowly we drew nearer to those buildings, and finally we clambered up the steep bank, to the village, the post, and Mr. Maver's home. Several Eskimos came hurrying to help the driver with the dogs and the unloading. I followed Mr. Maver through a snow porch, a sort of short tunnel about seven feet high, built to keep the snow from drifting against the door.

I had reached the goal of my winter journey—the real beginning of Eskimo land.

The region about Great Whale River in Quebec is broken and rocky—wooded in the valleys, bare and rugged on the hilltops. Of all the posts I visited, this proved the most interesting. It was really an overlapping of the more northern forests and the true Arctic, for a few Eskimos in coastal environments lived south of here, and some Indians lived north of the post, where there was still some forest. Each cultural group sought the surroundings their history had taught them to harmonize with; here at Great Whale River both Indians and Eskimos came to trade their fur. Even the Eskimos out on the Belcher Islands, about seventy miles off the coast, came over the winter ice to trade. On those treeless islands they had found the true Arctic—the Eskimo environment.

The same overlapping applied to the wildlife. Arctic forms appeared south of here; southern forms extended far to the north. Some species, such as the arctic hare, like the Eskimo, sought the open country. The varying hare, or snowshoe rabbit, like the Indian, preferred the forest. Each kind sought the habitat it had learned to survive in.

One day, as I was crossing the top of a rocky hill, I spied several rock ptarmigan squatting in the snow. I opened the Graflex camera and approached the nearest one. The image on the ground glass grew larger and larger, and finally I released the shutter. Still the bird did not move. Again I moved forward, and this time came so near I could hardly focus. I released the shutter. The bird was still sitting there! When I again drew nearer, the ptarmigan finally began to walk off in the snow. How tame could a wild bird be!

Another day I was tramping over the backcountry on snowshoes when I came across a fox track. A wild animal's trail always fascinated me, so I followed it a way. I just wanted to see what the fox had been doing, and the trail in the snow would tell me.

That evening I told the folks at the trading post what I had seen. Harold, a Scandinavian who was one of the hired help at the post, showed an eager interest in my story and wanted to know where the track was. I wondered about his keen interest in natural history. Next morning he went out for a few hours—and came back with a silver fox! Thus I learned about the perseverance and skill of these hunters. However, I got something out of my fox trail, too: Harold was glad to have me make a sketch of his fox before he skinned it.

How different Great Whale River seemed from the last time I had been here, in another season. Mr. Maver and his assistant, Mr. Renouf, assisted my work in many ways. I spent the time busily, making short excursions into the backcountry, getting a few specimens, painting watercolor pictures of birds, and—the happiest experience of all—getting acquainted with the people.

A new variation in my sojourn came when, with Mr. Maver's help, I took two Eskimo boys up the river a few miles for a five-day camping trip. By this time I had learned some Eskimo words and could carry on a little conversation. But we didn't need to talk. As we went snowshoeing off from the post, I on the long, slender type called "gillies" and the boys on their little round ones, they were striding along with big smiles on their young faces. There are times when we don't need words.

Leaving the camp we established, we came upon many rock ptarmigan, crossed weasel and lemming tracks, and discovered where an otter had been playing in the snow. It impressed me that in the summer, when I was on salary, I had felt an obligation to the museum, and with some exceptions my journal consisted largely of factual, scientific observations. Now, when I was on my own, I recorded more of my impressions and reactions to the events of this big natural world. While in this camp, on April 3, I made the following attempt to express some of my feelings:

"We met a sociable pair of Hudsonian chickadees, who came up close to us when I chirped. One of them would occasionally give vent to his cheerfulness with a little song-like trill. Surely spring is coming in earnest now! A little farther on we saw two pine grosbeaks flying off, and four redpolls; then three Canada jays. These are perfect days, living a free and easy camp life amid perfect surroundings—and spring is coming on!"

In a few days the boys and I were back at the trading post. At the store I asked them what they wanted for helping me in camp. One chose a mouth organ, the other a jumping jack.

Still, not all was pleasant at Great Whale River. One day I learned how desperate life up north can be. A young Indian staggered into the trading post, nearly dead from starvation. His family, camped far back in the forest, had run out of food, and he and his brother had started out for the trading post. His brother was carrying a muzzle-loading gun in hope of getting some ptarmigan along the way, but he accidentally lost the contents of the powder horn, so he could shoot nothing. Yet they struggled on, hoping to make it to the post or find someone. Finally the brother could go no farther, and this young one went on alone. His brother was out there about a mile, he thought.

People from the village hurried out and found the Indian, but he was dead. The other boy finally recovered, but I never did learn what happened to the family back in the woods.

This was a hungry country. I learned to eat hawks, owls, seabirds— anything that had meat on it. The Indians up here lived a most rugged life; yet they somehow had a kind view of nature, like the hunters who begged the bear's pardon before shooting it. They were a humble people.

One day an Indian brought us a big chunk of meat. Someone had been lucky enough to kill a caribou. It had evidently been brought a long way, for it smelled terrible from decay. But Mr. Maver, who was accustomed to such problems, trimmed away the smelly outside, and in the center was enough wholesome meat for a nice roast, which we all enjoyed.

I had one little difficulty of another kind. I had bought an arctic fox from an Eskimo, paying him the price he would get at the post. Someone higher up heard about this and felt I should pay to the Eskimo the price the Hudson's Bay Company would get in London. Apparently someone suspected I was going into fur-buying, in opposition to the company. But I could not afford that kind of business. That was the only fur I bought, and I finally won the argument.

Following some instructions given me by Mr. Renouf, I learned one day about another Indian custom. Out on the beach I found a simple heap of boulders. Being curious, and rather bold I suppose, I pushed away the larger of the boulders and there found the remains of an Indian baby, tightly sewed into a coarse fabric. There was no marker of any kind. So this was the way they disposed of human remains! I carefully replaced every boulder just as I had found it.

One day in March some Eskimos came over the ice from the Belcher Islands to trade their furs, and another group arrived from up north somewhere. I began to see more Eskimos in the village, and my thoughts went longingly northward. One morning I watched an Eskimo family loading their dogsled to go back up north. There was a little child bundled up safely on top of the load. The mother pulled up a few plants of heather, or crowberry, which carries its black berries through the winter. These she placed on the load in front of the little child, so there would be something to eat as they traveled along. Would I see these people again? As they moved away out onto the ice, I thought more than ever about going on north.

On March 20, my brother Martin's birthday, my thoughts went southward, to our home in Minnesota—to another world. How was my family getting along? Here I was, on a long adventure with no income, and I wondered how my younger brother was doing, supporting the household. That home, so far away, was close and dear in my thoughts. But there could be no turning back in this far country. I was spending a year on my own and planning to get still farther north

Nastapoka and Northward

The harder the winter, the more welcome the spring! February had been a severe month. For the traveler it was a month of strain and tension, a continual struggle against the cold, biting wind sweeping down across the ice and against blinding snowstorms. For the Eskimo there was the task of making a living, which consisted of hunting seal day after day under discouraging conditions. Winter was at the pinnacle of its power in February.

Then came March. The air was still cold, and snowstorms still swept down from the north, but somehow the snap of midwinter was gone; the north wind had lost its cutting edge. There were days when the sun shone warmly, with an occasional breeze from the south. The distant woods acquired a softer blue. We felt that winter was slipping away and rejoiced at the prospect of spring.

April brought the first real signs. The snow softened until at times snowshoeing became difficult. The wild creatures, too, responded to the season's promise. Pine grosbeaks were singing—a trilling, bubbling, happy song in a land still covered with snow! But that is the way of the North. The whiskey jacks (gray jays) became very furtive and silent now—no doubt they were already nesting. On April 5 I saw the first bird arrivals from the south, a small band of snow buntings. A week later a ptarmigan appeared with brown feathers in its snow-white plumage. No doubt about spring now.

The Eskimos were arriving from along the coast to trade their furs. One brought me for a specimen a white, woolly baby seal. The young of the harbor seal are born out on the ice in March, clothed in a temporary white fur. In a very short time this is shed and the new dark coat appears.

As I watched the Eskimo families going back up north, I wanted to go too. On April 27 it happened. A satisfactory arrangement was made with Wetunnok and Pootuok for me to accompany them to their summer hunting grounds at the mouth of the Nastapoka River; that would place me in the midst of the territory I wanted to investigate. I could explore the area while waiting for the breakup of the ice. So, late in the day two dogsleds were loaded with all our gear and supplies, with a large canoe lashed on top of one of them for use later, and we were off to real Eskimo land!

I should explain that the Eskimo I was to live with did not know a word of English. But Reverend Walton, whose headquarters were at Fort George, had given me the Eskimo phrase *Shu-now-na* ("what is the name of that?"). Armed with this and the very few other words I had picked up, I set forth with my two companions.

In the usual Hudson Bay manner, we all trotted along beside the sleds. From out on the bay the world looked white. To the west, snow-covered ice extended to the far low horizon; to the east, it was white to the shore, then snow-covered trees on into the interior of Labrador. This was the world we were headed for, the Eskimos and I, as we trekked northward, toward their little village near Nastapoka River.

I felt at first, out there on the ice, that it was a plain, white, lifeless prospect in all directions—where we had come from, and where we were going. Then a bit of life appeared above the white, over toward the shore— a black raven flapping along. It was a dark, living accent in what seemed a blank, white world. I was moved by this spot of life, and I knew the raven's name in Eskimo. "*Toolualuk!*" I exclaimed to Wetunnok, pointing.

"*Ai! Ai!*" he responded, his face breaking into vivacious smiles.

That was the extent of our conversation: "Raven!" and a vehement "Yes! Yes!" But the barrier was broken; we had said something to each other!

I looked back at the raven disappearing in the distance. Where was he going? We know that every creature has to eat. Even the plants that I knew were hidden under the snow on the shore. What was the raven finding to eat up here in this snow-covered northern world? I supposed he could go a long time without food—we all can, for that matter, if only we realize it—but there has to be something, sometime. The raven disappeared, and I thought of other things.

As the days went on, I learned what it was to travel in comfort. The snow had melted off the ice by this time, which made the going smooth; the dogs swung along at a rapid gait, and we could sit on the load as much as we pleased. Day after day the sun came out, warm and bright. Birds coming north swooped by us in flocks. We were passing varied landscapes now, too—no longer a blank, white world. When we traveled near the shore, dark, rocky islands loomed up from the ice. On the mainland granite hills appeared, changing farther on to smooth, sloping areas of solid rock, cut with chasms and rising in steep cliffs farther inland. We passed a number of interesting little streams cutting their way through the rock. This was real travel, with plenty of time and a relaxed atmosphere. Sometimes the Eskimos would stop to shoot a seal.

At Richmond Gulf we found a small encampment, where my guides had left their families. Here was quite a stretch of open water. Rather than going all the way around, we launched the canoe and ferried across the sleds, dogs, supplies, and Eskimo families. And here I saw a welcome sight: seagulls flying over the water.

Richmond Gulf is a large, picturesque piece of water, almost a salt-water lake. It is connected to Hudson Bay by a narrow channel called Gulf Hazard, which is a well-known landmark. It is a dangerous place to navigate at certain times, for the tide rushes in and out with terrific speed. Here we approached the northern limit of trees. Southward as far as Great Whale River, the forest is thin and confined mostly to the valleys with bare hilltops raising their rocky crowns everywhere. On the immediate shores of Richmond Gulf, the spruce groves attain a respectable size, but north of this point the forest is represented only by very small clumps of twisted, stunted trees here and there. Sometimes they are merely a low, spreading, mosslike mat of branches, with a trunk little more than a foot high. Then even these vestiges disappear, and the land is truly Arctic.

The snow was melting rapidly, and the land was becoming bare. I walked on the shore while the sleds moved slowly along on the ice. After so much snow and ice, the earth and rock felt good underfoot. On such occasions I saw snowy owls on rocky points and small groups of ptarmigan. One day I heard the sweet, welcome song of a tree sparrow in a little patch of willows. Twice I spied an arctic hare crouching beside a big stone. The hares were still white, conspicuous on the bare ground.

Early one afternoon the Eskimos turned in to the land and prepared to make camp. "*Pa-tuk-tok*," Wetunnok announced, pointing to a river not too far away.

This was his name for the Nastapoka River; here was to be my camp for some time. I soon perceived that I would have plenty of neighbors. In the next day or two one sled after another arrived, until there were at least nine or ten tents in our little village.

Day after day I was learning more of the language. These simple, childlike people, who spoke not a word of English, were eager to teach me the Eskimo language. And they showed wonderful ability to understand the blunderings of a white man trying to pronounce their guttural words.

I soon was aware that they called me *Kopinua angoraka* ("little-bird white man"). They had watched me preparing specimens!

I had little trouble with nouns but had difficulty understanding their adjectives. Often, for instance, a woman would come over to my tent and ask if I wanted water. If I did not want to be bothered, I would say "*E-muk amisoot.*" I thought I was saying "plenty of water," but I often noticed a smile on the woman's face. One day, when the two Eskimo guides and I were out in the canoe, Wetunnok undertook to explain to me the difference between *angiok* and *amisoot*. He talked until the sweat poured out on his face, but still I couldn't understand.

Then Pootuok, who was in the bow, turned to me and undertook the task. He used the word *imak* which means "thus" or "like this." He spread one hand out flat and made a lot of points on it with the other, saying, "*Amisoot imak.*" Then he swung both arms in a big sweep and said, "*Angiok imak!*"

As he said "*Angiok*" his deep voice expressed to me his idea, and I got the meaning. *Amisoot* was "many," *angiok* was "much" or "big." I had been saying "many water"—no wonder the woman had smiled!

Another day when I had learned a little Eskimo, Wetunnok and I were out on the ice near an island. He asked me, "*Kaht-sik ahput-peete-hunge-tok-tekko-lauk-reet?*" ("How many snow-there-is-none have you seen?" or "How old are you?")

I understood him and replied, "*ahwettinget pingashurroktut.*" But I forgot to add the syllable *lo* which means "and." So instead of saying "Twenty and six," I had said, "Twenty sixes."

Wetunnok laughed merrily, for he understood my mistake, and I laughed, too, when I suddenly realized what I had said.

Much has been said and written about the filth of the Eskimo, and I found nothing to cause me to dispute such statements. They may wash their faces sometimes, but I never caught them at it. (I don't remember washing mine very often either!) Not all the "cooties" were in the trenches of France, for the Eskimos were well supplied. I often saw young girls picking over one another's hair, and when one of them made a find, I was amazed to see her pop it into her mouth! I thought of monkeys I had seen in the zoo, doing the very same thing.

But filth was only one item in Eskimo life. Many of their other qualities are admirable characteristics which more civilized beings would do well to emulate. The Eskimo was always cheerful and good-natured. You might come into a camp that had been fasting for several days, but you would not guess the fact from their countenances. You would be greeted by the brief, energetic *Ai!* or *Chimo*, the Eskimo "hello," accompanied by a smile and a firm handshake. They would tell you in due time that they were hungry, but they would be pleasant about it and go into an ecstasy of childish delight over any little morsel you could give them. I have never seen a people so contented in the face of adversity and so filled with gratitude for small favors.

The Eskimos were good neighbors, very helpful to one another. If a hunter was successful, he did not hoard his game but shared it with the rest of the camp. They were especially kind to a white stranger. The only firewood we had at this camp was the driftwood picked up along the beach; it was gleaned on the seaward shore of the island especially, and hauled in on the sleds, sometimes a distance of two or more miles. But my tent was always well supplied.

How can I tell of all the significant incidents in my life with these Eskimos? On one occasion I spied an arctic hare, pure white, on a rocky slope some distance away. Wetunnok joined me as I hurried to my tent for the camera and started back. Before we were halfway to the hare, a shot rang out, and the animal bounded away. A small boy with a shotgun arose from behind a rock. I expressed my disappointment, and Wetunnok, thinking I was displeased with the boy, gave him a severe scolding. The boy, of course, had been doing his best to serve me, thinking I would want the hare's skin above all else. Both of them took up the chase, promising me that they would find the animal for me. And they did! After a long search the hare was again seen, snuggling down into a rocky nook. This time I secured the picture, and we were all satisfied.

One day, when I was away, some dogs got into my tent and ate some ptarmigan skins I had assembled. The skins were all poisoned with arsenic to keep moths out, but that didn't seem to bother the dogs. But Wetunnok was upset. Finally he assured me that he could take me inland to where I could get all the ptarmigan I wanted. So we planned an overnight trip, and that first evening reached a place where, as he had promised, ptarmigan were plentiful. There we planned to spend the night.

Wetunnok had a young boy with him. There were still some snow-drifts, and at one of these they proceeded to build an igloo. The boy brought the snow blocks to Wetunnok, who expertly built a dome-shaped igloo, complete with a short runway into the door.

We had with us only a very thin blanket apiece. When the time came we rolled into them and went to sleep with all our clothes on. During the night, when my circulation slowed down, the snowy atmosphere chilled me awake. I had to warm up with a wakeful circulation before I could doze off again for a bit. Each time, I looked across at my two companions, sleeping peacefully through the whole night! This was my only experience in a snow igloo, and the following evening I was happy to crawl into my warm rabbit-skin bag in my own tent.

Another time I was out on the ice with Wetunnok when he was after seals. We saw one—a dark object off in the distance. Wetunnok instructed me to stand in front of the dogteam and brandish a long limber whip. He would stalk the seal. When Wetunnok went off, I did as I had been told.

I stood in front of the dogs, sliding the long lash back and forth over the ice. But the dogs were restless—who was this fellow in front of them who did not use the Eskimo commands they were used to? One and then another would tentatively lunge, anxious to follow his master. It was all I could do to intimidate them enough with the whip to keep them there.

Then a shot rang out. The team leapt forward; I flopped onto the sled as it sped past me, and we had a wild ride all the way to where Wetunnok was standing over a dead seal. The dogs rushed up and greedily licked the blood off the ice. Apparently that was their share of the hunt, and they knew it.

On another day Wetunnok and I were again out on the ice, this time walking without a dogteam. And by now there were cracks in the ice—open leads of water here and there. We came to one, and my companion jumped across. I too jumped, but encumbered by the parka I was wearing, I fell partly into the water on the far side.

"*Ak-pai-nes!*" Wetunnok cried, running to me. His white man was in trouble! But I clambered out easily by myself.

As we went on over the ice, there occurred one of the beautiful incidents of spring in the Arctic which lingers in my memory as a striking picture of that ice wonderland. We came to a wide-open lane of water. There were some birds there, and Wetunnok remarked, "*Metiuk* ('Eider')." We went a little closer. There were the eiders, some in the water, others up on the ice edge; and out in the middle, on a floating bit of "iceberg," perched two glaucous gulls.

Color? There was the dark water, the edges of the ice in various shades of blue-green, white of the ice surface beyond, the white and light blue gull, the colorful eiders swimming and sitting on the ice edge. In my mind our walk on the sea ice was a success, a day to remember.

A northern spring is varied and unaccountable. The birds were nesting, plants were sprouting, and already a charming little purple flower, the mountain saxifrage, was blooming everywhere over the rocks. Yet we were to have one more snowstorm. On June 8 I sat all day in my little tent, listening to the raging wind and the monotonous flapping of the canvas. The windward wall bulged in threateningly, and I was in constant fear that the ropes would snap and my whole outfit would be scattered over the landscape. It was a northeast wind, with driving snow. When I looked out, the ground was once more white, the tents ghostly in a gray, whirling mist. Altogether it was a dreary outlook after the bright sunny promises of spring. I ducked back into my straining, flapping tent and crawled into the blankets.

Suddenly a couple of ropes of the tent snapped, but some Eskimos came immediately to fix them and prevent collapse. An Eskimo family was not so fortunate. Their tent suddenly lay flat on the ground, household goods flying in all directions. But everyone rushed out to help, and there was a great scramble to gather all the things in the storm. Finally the tent was pitched in a more sheltered spot back of a rocky knoll.

Later in the afternoon some boys came to inform me that there were "*Kopinua amisoot* ('Small birds, many')." I crawled out to investigate. There were indeed struggling groups of tree sparrows and other small birds striving to find bits to eat in the shelter of bushes, rocks, and little tufts of grass. Beaten here and there, they were having a fearful time of it. They could hardly keep a foothold on the ground and were in danger of being blown out to sea. I went back to my shelter, wishing the day were done and yet dreading the night.

Toward evening Wetunnok poked his head into my tent and announced, "*Siko aud-lat*! ('The ice is going!')" Once more I crawled out to see for myself. Through the snow-driven air I saw dull black water, rolling in billows and lashed into vicious whitecaps—a strange sight after so many months of white expanse.

A few days after the storm, the ground was once more bare of snow. The little purple flowers were sprightly as ever, seemingly none the worse for their bath of snow. Birds were again beginning to sing, but we continued to find them dead here and there, victims of the storm. I wondered how many had blown away to perish in open water.

The Eskimos were busy making their kayaks now, for the dogsleds were put away for another season. The men shaped the framework from choice bits of driftwood, the whole construction being fastened with seal-skin thongs. When the framework was completed, the whole community concentrated on one kayak at a time. The women gathered about the frame and sewed on the wet, flabby sealskins. This was an occasion for great hilarity and a general good time. When completely covered with skins, the kayak was elevated on stakes to dry and to keep it out of reach of dogs. The skins were sewed so cleverly that after they dried and tightened like drumheads, the seams were perfectly watertight.

I had my own reason to realize how efficient those women were. During the spring and summer I wore knee-high, watertight sealskin boots. After several days of wading about in the wet grass and moist ground, these boots became misshapen and hard when dried. One day when I came back to camp, having worn other footgear, I found that some woman had found my hardened sealskin boots and chewed them soft and pliable! No wonder the Eskimos had strong jaws and perfect, strong teeth!

These people of the Arctic had heard about the war that was raging in Europe. It was going strong then, in 1915. Wetunnok once asked me who was fighting over there. How was I to explain to him the various nations then trying to kill each other off? Finally I had an idea. I had a few cans of corned beef, on whose wrappers were instructions in English, French, and German. I pointed to the three instructions in turn and said, "These two are fighting this one."

That was the best I could do, but Wetunnok nodded his head. He knew that each nation had a language; and what did it matter who they were?

One day the ice floes came back close to the land, and next morning I saw dark blobs here and there on the white surface—seals on the ice. Eskimos up on rocky points were watching them through the cheap telescopes they had obtained at the trading post. But no one seemed to be doing anything more than this.

Finally Wetunnok came to my tent. "Why don't you people go out after seals?" I asked.

"This is Sunday," he replied. Here was the influence of the missionary in the Eskimo wilderness. I hesitated to apply any adverse pressure, but finally I said, "Didn't Mr. Walton tell you that necessary work can be done on Sunday?"

"Yes, he told us that. But we don't want to do it anyway." Then I recognized that modern hypocrisy was entering in. The Eskimos thought their abstinence would find favor with this white man.

"Wetunnok, your families, your children are hungry. They need food.

Tell your people to go out and get some seals!" He went away without a word. Presently one kayak went out, then another, and then some more. They got plenty of seals.

This same viewpoint was shown another time. I had obtained a muskrat, skinned it, and was preparing the specimen in my tent. Wetunnok came in on one of his frequent visits. "Wetunnok, do your people want this meat?"

He looked at me questioningly, and finally said, "No, we don't eat that kind of meat."

I knew very well that they ate any kind of meat. I replied, "All right, then I will eat it myself."

He looked at me with surprise, and then went quietly away.

But these people had something we should admire, a trait they share with other peoples on the far frontier. They were honest! I had a good supply of food, including several sacks of flour. Most of the flour was to give to the Eskimos, but I could not support so many families. I could only give each of them a little now and then, in order to make it last.

But I could go away all day, time after time, and nothing was ever touched. Once I came back from a day afield to find that my tent had been moved to a fresh place—and all my supplies had been moved. Not a thing had been taken.

Was it because I trusted them? I don't know.

NOW THAT THE ICE HAD BROKEN UP, IT WAS TIME FOR ME TO MOVE ON again. My preparations were simple: I packed all my specimens into wooden boxes and stored them in one of the Eskimo tents. Taking what supplies we needed, Wetunnok, Pootuok, and I launched a canoe one afternoon in June and started up the coast. This was to be the last lap of my journey. Port Harrison, the Revillon Frères Company trading post near Portland Promontory, was my objective. It was to be my "farthest north."

We were favored with good weather day after day, an unusual state of affairs on Hudson Bay. These summer days were bright and very long. The sun set in the north, almost within an hour of midnight, and a few hours later arose a little to the east of north. The sunset colors lingered on the northern horizon until they merged into sunrise. I hardly knew when to go to bed—my days were very long. Paddling, stopping at every interesting place along the shore, making camp and exploring from each camp for perhaps hours—the days were brimming with interest for me, the culmination of my long journey. This strip of coast between Nastapoka and Port Harrison had been my goal; my purpose was to explore it and study the nesting birds. Now the weather and the June daylight promised me success.

Sometimes we followed the mainland shore closely, but occasionally we crossed over to the Nastapoka Islands, which lie in a long chain parallel to the coast, a mile or more away. On the steep cliffs of these islands, we found the nests of ravens, duck hawks, and glaucous gulls. As we rounded rocky points, eiders would swim away in stately style. Snow buntings had built their nests up among the rocks, and the male birds sang cheerily from their perches on boulders.

One day we came to a low island above which a colony of herring gulls circled, cackling in alarm at our approach. I went ashore to investigate the nests. The Eskimos came along with a tin pail. After exploring the island and making notes on the nests—number of eggs, etc.—I took three or four eggs for my dinner and returned to the canoe. I had selected eggs from nests containing only a few, to make sure they were fresh and not to interfere with the nesting.

Presently the Eskimos came back, Wetunnok carrying a pail full of eggs. They had robbed nearly every nest on the island! I tried to make them understand that I was displeased with such wholesale robbing of birds' nests when other food was at hand. They pretended to agree with my sentiments, but I knew that when they were by themselves they would wipe out any bird colony they came across, for an Eskimo cannot resist going ashore when eggs are in view. When they cooked their pail of eggs, they found many of them partly incubated; some contained well-formed young, but that made no difference to Wetunnok and Pootuok!

While we were busy at the island, loose pieces of ice had been drifting in with the tide, and we were almost cut off from the shore. We hurriedly paddled off, picking our way through open lanes of water, and were almost through the ice when we found the passage before us again blocked. Other ice hemmed us in behind now, and we were trapped, with large ice cakes grinding and encroaching on all sides. The guides immediately headed for the largest piece of ice and climbed out on it. With a desperate effort we hauled the heavily loaded canoe up onto the ice. We slid it across and shoved off into the water on the other side. Here, by chance, we found one open channel and paddled out of danger.

"*Nekugmik! Nekugmik!*" Wetunnok exclaimed. "Thanks! Thanks!" I have never forgotten his words. He felt grateful that the universe had saved him, and he expressed his gratitude aloud. The feeling of relief at our escape from the situation was more exciting than the crisis itself. I realized then how easily one may be caught napping. The guides had been earnest and silent, but now that it was over, they became talkative and laughed like children.

The coast was not uninhabited. On several occasions we passed small Eskimo encampments. We always stopped to pass the time of day, and the guides promptly absorbed all the local gossip. As we paddled up to one such camp, an old woman came running down to the beach shouting, "*Tobacco-mik! Tobacco-mik!*" She had a piece of a pipe stem which she was mouthing in lieu of tobacco. Her happiness was pathetic when I gave her a plug of the black tobacco I carried with me to give away. The whole encampment gathered around, and one or two leading citizens carried on a conversation with my guides. Wetunnok at once assumed a very lordly air, as befits a guide! Most of the others stood silent, with pursed lips and attentive eyes, taking in the conversation. One young woman, standing on a rock, carried a child on her back, with its head peeking out from the hood of her parka. She swayed from foot to foot in regular rhythm, constantly flapping the sides of the hood to keep the mosquitoes from annoying her little "papoose"—for mosquitoes were now out in swarms.

Each time, when we had said good-bye all around and were once more in the canoe, my guides would tell me, bit by bit, the information they had gathered. So-and-so (unpronounceable) had shot an *oog-rook*, or bearded seal, day before yesterday. Someone had seen four caribou back in the hills. There had not been tobacco in camp for a long time—and so forth. There was evidently no politics nor economics to talk about, so their conversation centered on the hunt and personal, neighborly gossip.

Spring was at its best now. The days were really warm and pleasant. Birds were singing and nesting, and a variety of wildflowers bloomed in profusion on the shores, above the pretty little beaches with their strips of tide-washed sand bordered by a band of rich green. Could this be the bleak, barren North of snow and ice I had once known?

One day as we passed between two islands with steep, towering cliffs on either side, we made a sound that came back to us in a double echo. That started the Eskimos laughing. Wetunnok shouted something, listened for the two distinct replies of the echo, then roared with laughter. He gave shout after shout, and he and Pootuok laughed till the tears ran. That got me started! I heard my first English words in a long time, as they came bouncing back to me from those high rock bluffs. We must have been a comical sight—three men in a canoe, playing with Echo like little boys.

After passing around two more islands, Wetunnok pointed out a group of buildings on the distant shore. Port Harrison! I was expecting to reach it sometime that day, but our arrival seemed so sudden. It was June 27. We had started from Nastapoka on the 21st, so we had made very good time, considering the many stops we had made along the way.

As we drew into the shore below the trading post, Mr. Herodias, the trader, came hurrying down the slope to welcome us. For the first time in months, aside from the visit with Echo, I could speak my own language. I had arrived at my "farthest north."

Port Harrison, located near the mouth of the Innuksuak River, looked like a lonely place. Bare, rocky slopes extend away behind the post to higher hills, which at this place are some distance back from the coast, leaving the immediate surroundings rather low and comparatively level. There are of course no trees. Opposite the buildings lies an interesting group of islands.

The steamer sent out by the Revillon Frères Trading Company, usually the only link with the rest of the world, called at this post only once a year with supplies and mail. When the steamer would leave, the two men left at the post had a whole year in which to read their letters and study the batch of ancient newspapers. Occasionally a dogteam went down the coast in winter to the Revillon Frères Company post at Fort George, a distance of several hundred miles. The mail brought in at such times helped to break the long monotony.

Mr. Ward, the young English assistant at this post, complained of the isolation and the long winters. He was evidently glad to see a visitor who had more recent news from the outside world. I was shown a variety of handy little contrivances about the house, which they had carved from wood during long winter months. Occasionally a few caribou or a polar bear afforded a little hunting. This spring, apparently to make matters worse, the supply of tobacco was very low and would hardly last until ship time. The young fellow declared, however, that he would "stick" for two years more and fulfill his contract.

Mr. Ward also told me an interesting little tale about the Eskimos. On its last trip, the steamer had brought several sheep to the post. They died; the meat spoiled, and the animals were buried. But sometime later the Eskimos dug them up and ate the meat!

In spite of the fine hospitality at Port Harrison, I knew I must be getting south again. On June 29, after only one day there, we said good-bye to these friendly people.

The first trip over new country is the most interesting, I suppose. Traveling northward, there had been the incentive of exploring new places—strange rivers, islands, and rocky hills. I had watched eagerly for all the Arctic bird life—the snow buntings, eider ducks, and more obscure species—all on their ancestral breeding grounds. I had hunted the steep cliffs for nests of ravens and peregrine falcons, and all the little lakes for waterbirds. My notebook was being filled with scientific data.

Of course I still observed, recorded, and collected specimens on the way south, but fascinating as the country was, my thoughts began to reach out toward my destination: the little home in Minnesota. Even the two Eskimos, who were used to the treeless Arctic, began to speak in glowing terms of Richmond Gulf, where firewood was so plentiful!

Luck was still with us; we had good weather. One day we had a strong wind at our backs and ordinarily the Eskimo would not venture out in a canoe among the resulting waves. But there were enough small ice floes scattered over the water to prevent waves from forming, so we put up a sail and went merrily on our way among the ice floes! At Port Harrison we had learned that the ice had gone off just a few days before our arrival.

On the way north, while we were paddling along the shore of an island, I had smelled something rotten but could not at first locate it. Then I heard one of the Eskimos say, "We'll wait until we come back south again." A moment later I had spied it—a dead seal, awash at the water's edge. Several days later, as we were passing this same place, the seal still lay there, but other Eskimos had been there and had taken several big slabs of meat off one side. If my two Eskimo friends had been by themselves, I am sure they would have helped themselves to some tasty morsels. Life isn't the same everywhere, is it?

After a few pleasant days we were back at the camp at Nastapoka, and my Eskimo companions could again be with their families. This camp had been my home for many weeks that spring; I found it a homey, familiar place, where I had had many fine experiences with these friendly people. But I was anxious to connect with the steamer at Great Whale River, and Wetunnok and Pootuok were to take me there in the canoe.

On the day we were to leave to go on south, Wetunnok came to me and explained that he wanted me to come see a woman in a certain tent. He said she was about to leave this world, and she wanted me to say good-bye to her. When we went into the tent, I saw a woman lying face down, her forehead resting on a rolled-up cylindrical bolster. When I came in, she raised her head and smiled at me warmly. She knew she was dying. I hardly knew what to say, but I felt so kindly toward her and very sincerely, I said my good-bye to her in Eskimo. I left the tent feeling sad and helpless.

Then came the launching from the shore—the good-bye to Nastapoka. I knew I might never again see this part of the country, with its beautiful natural surroundings. I had disposed of my surplus supplies and kept in the canoe just enough to see us down to Great Whale River. The whole village lined up along the shore to see us off. One old woman came hurrying over to give me a going-away present—a small roll of sinew. I still have it, and I treasure it for the friendly motivation that went with that gift. I shook hands with each one. As we got into the canoe and paddled off there was a waving of hands, a circle of friendly smiles, and a chorus of "*Chimo! Aksunai!*"—an Eskimo farewell.

When we reached Richmond Gulf, we stopped to camp one night at its entrance. As I walked toward a grove of trees, I heard the full-throated chirp of a robin. Surely this was a greeting from home! A little later, the robin treated me to his whole song. At the same time, white whales—the belugas—were going in and out of the gulf, following the tide. Here was a mingling of the Arctic and more southern elements.

A few days later, farther down the coast, we saw human footprints on the sand of a beach. "*Adlait* ('Indian')," Wetunnok assured me, explaining that only the Indians go barefoot at this time of year. So we were back in Indian country! During the next few days we stopped at several Indian camps where all of the people were barefoot.

On July 15, a calm, bright morning, we paddled in to Great Whale River. It was heartwarming to be greeted again by Mr. Maver and the other friends I had enjoyed on the way north in the winter. My "farthest north" venture was over. There was a delightful accumulation of mail there for me, too, brought up by dogteams in the spring. And I learned at once that the *Inenew* had not yet arrived, so I had not missed my transportation.

Wetunnok and Pootuok felt they must start back north the very next morning. I paid them off by letting them get goods at the store, charged on my letter of credit with the Hudson's Bay Company. Then it was good-bye once more. These two represented my last contact with such a different way of life. I had learned their language, learned to live as they did, and learned much of their viewpoint. As we shook hands there in front of the store and they walked away from me, I felt I was saying good-bye to a rare experience.

While waiting at Great Whale River, I had a chance to review in my thoughts the significance of my sojourn with those friendly people at Nastapoka and beyond. Wetunnok had been my most constant companion and had answered my numerous questions. As I had tramped over the country around Nastapoka, I noticed little masses of white fox fur here and there. One day when Wetunnok and I were out together on the shore, we came on one of these, and I asked him what he thought about it. He assured me that an arctic fox had died here, and another starving fox had found the body and eaten it.

We often take it for granted that the lemming is a unique animal in that it has population crises. But the population cycle is common to many other animals. That winter the ptarmigan were very scarce in some parts of Hudson Bay. At Moose Factory the snowshoe rabbit had reached the peak of its numbers and was dying off everywhere. We now know that this rabbit has a cycle which reaches abundance every ten or eleven years. The lynx follows the pattern of the rabbit. In times of scarcity, the lynx has been known to eat its own young—comparable to the cannibalism I had learned about that winter. I had found lemmings extremely scarce along the Hudson Bay coast, a fact which partly explained those piles of arctic fox fur.

One day, as we sat on a hill near Nastapoka River, Wetunnok told me of the time when he was starving. He pointed out to me the kinds of grasses he had eaten to keep alive during that time. He told it all in a matter-of-fact way, the same matter-of-fact manner I had noticed in other Eskimos when they were short of food.

Thinking over my experiences with those Eskimos and their attitudes in the face of adversity, I have come to certain conclusions. I am reminded of an incident across the continent, at Nome, Alaska, related by Sally Carrighar in her book, *Moonlight at Midday*. A missionary, new to the country, was asking an Eskimo woman whether they had laws among them. The Eskimo woman is reported as replying, "No." Speaking to Sally afterward, she said, "After all, we know the difference between right and wrong!"

As I think of my sojourn among the Eskimos of Hudson Bay, I realize that there was no law there—no officers in uniform. People reacted to each other in a natural way.

We, as humans, have certainly not reached our human goal; we are only on the way. I am convinced that in the evolution of the human spirit something much worse than hunger can happen to a people.

I HAD MANY FORTUNATE INCIDENTS IN MY HUDSON BAY ADVENTURE, AND here was another. During my absence from Great Whale River, some Eskimo coming over the ice from the Belcher Islands had reported that a steamer was stranded out there, in pretty good condition. This report had gone down to Moose Factory. So when the *Inenew* arrived at Great Whale River in August, she was prepared to go out and salvage the ship if possible, and I was permitted to accompany the party.

On the evening of August 14, we pulled into a harbor along the rocky shores of South Belcher Island. The next day we steamed along the coast of the island to another harbor, where we found an Eskimo camp and obtained information about the steamer, stranded somewhere to the westward.

I wasn't much interested in the steamer. I wanted to roam over the island and see what was there. Here were Eskimos again, some of whom had never seen white men before. They were living their lives out there on those treeless islands, living largely off the sea as primitive Eskimos do. Their only contact with the trading post was through a few of them who traveled over the ice in winter.

The tents of this village were all made of sealskin. Apparently they heard of my interest in artifacts, and some of them brought me old harpoon points, which they called *tsavili*. One day I came upon something which revealed more of their customs to me—about a dozen graves, nine of them grouped together. They were square, with walls of stone and flat rocks over the top. Over some of the larger tombs were small logs of driftwood laid across as rafters, on which stones were placed. In many cases bits of wood from kayaks lay about, pieces of the circular frame around the opening of the kayak. That was all. In this simple way they cared for their dead.

Once, when I had been out all day, I returned to the beach to find that the little ship's boat was out there with the anchored *Inenew*. I had no way to get back on board. I asked some of the Eskimos in the village if I could borrow a kayak to go out to the ship.

"*Ai!*" one of the young men said, and went with me to put a kayak into the water. Then, to my surprise, he got in and crawled feet first under the deck, with his face right in the bottom of the opening. When I got in, I found his face virtually in my lap. I took the double-bladed paddle and began to push off. After a few moments I realized that every time I lifted a blade to put the other one in the water for a stroke, water trickled down the handle and into the Eskimo's face. He didn't say a word, just blinked his eyes. Then I remembered that in using such a double paddle, the custom is to slide the handle back and forth on the sloping gunwale. When I did that, the water stopped dripping. I eventually got us out to the ship, and the Eskimo had a visit with some friends who were aboard.

One day after several of us had been ashore to explore, an Indian who was a member of the ship's crew reported an encounter with a polar bear. He had nothing but an old muzzle-loading double-barreled shotgun. When he saw the bear, he crept up to it and fired into its side. The bear gave a roar and started for the hunter. When the bear was only a few yards away, the Indian fired the other barrel, then turned and ran without being sure whether the bear was killed.

That evening we returned to the spot with a crew of Eskimos to skin the animal in case we should find him. They, of course, were to have the meat. When we reached the place of the shooting, we found nothing but a little blood. However, the ground was scratched up and a ragged trail led off.

We followed cautiously for several hundred yards, then spied a large white mass lying in a cleft in the rocks. The bear was still breathing, but a shot from my rifle made sure of him. The Eskimos were all busy immediately and soon had it skinned and the meat cut up. The next day the whole camp feasted on bear meat.

We waited many days in that harbor because of stormy weather, but we finally got out to the stranded ship, which we learned was the *Fort Churchill*. Apparently she had broken loose from her moorings on the west coast of Hudson Bay and had floated away without a crew. We marveled that the boat could drift all the way across Hudson Bay, and thread the many narrow passages of South Belcher Island and all its small outlying islands, to land finally in the protected spot where we found her—all with comparatively little damage. The Eskimos had carried off all loose articles and detachable parts, but otherwise the vessel was in good condition. After some days of work, we had her in tow in deep water. But due to the weather it took us several more days before we reached the sheltered anchorage of Great Whale River.

I had thought that I would have that polar bear skin and skull for the museum. But there were several high officials of the company aboard ship, and one of them thought the bear skin would make a fine trophy rug in his home. Who was I to object? I was there only by kind tolerance. So that bear never reached Carnegie Museum.

One day during that journey someone shot a loon, and the ship's cook decided to roast it. There were a good many disparaging remarks among the "outside" officials. Eat a loon? Of all things! However, when the meal was spread on the table, we all partook of it, and presently a very vocal official exclaimed, "I beg the loon's pardon! This is delicious!"

The Belchers are long, rocky islands, rising to an elevation of between two and three hundred feet. The coast is low in some places, but in others rocky with many cliffs. Back from the shores are numerous lakes, large and small, scattered over large areas of tundra. The numerous small islands are low, with gravelly beaches. Of the one large main island, where the village was, the Eskimos told us we could travel a whole day before we would come to the end of it. This was the northern part of the "South Belchers."

For a time now my life was spent mostly aboard ship. From Great Whale River we towed the rescued vessel southward, rode out rough weather in the lee of the islands, and finally on September 4, reached the little settlement on Charlton Island. I was left to make my way south, while the *Inenew* and her tow went on up the west coast of Hudson Bay to Churchill.

Here again I had a chance to collect specimens. Always specimens! I had to keep thinking of them, of somehow breaking even on this venture of mine. While I was camped at Charlton Island, Robert Flaherty and his schooner *Laddie* arrived from far north in the Struttons. I met Mrs. Flaherty, too. The only record of this meeting I find in my diary is on September 23: "Went up to the first lakes with Miss Thurston and Mrs. Flaherty, to take photos."

As one naturalist—I think it was Henry Van Dyke—said, "The best part of a trip is the part that escapes the notebook." Sometimes I find this is true. Certainly I was inspired by my time with the Flahertys, even though few words were written in my notebook.

To get over to Moose Factory I found passage on a little sailing ship, but the trip was a terrifically rough one. We barely made it to the post, arriving on September 26. I was thankful to arrive at this familiar place, to greet all the friends there, to stay in my room at the Moores' again, and to listen to Mrs. Moore's stories of Cree Indian customs.

For nearly three weeks I waited at Moose Factory for some kind of transportation. But I had the pleasure of going out on the tidal marshes of James Bay, which swarmed with waterfowl and other birds, and of visiting with all the people of the post to learn what had happened during the summer.

One day I learned that a sick Indian was being taken up to Cochrane for treatment. The packet with mail was being sent up, and I was invited to go along. So on October 18 we started up Moose River, three canoes of us. I was finally leaving Hudson Bay.

I suppose it is true that the best part of a trip escapes the notebook. But sometimes a journal entry brings back rich memories. My journal for that day, October 18, reads: "It was with feelings of regret that I said goodbye to all and saw Moose Factory disappear from view. But soon we were rounding picturesque points, new vistas opening up as we wound about among the islands of Moose River. The water is dark brown, the willows and poplars rich yellow and gold, set off with a background of dark spruce."

One more incident on this journey home lingers in memory. On the night of October 21, in the moonlight, I awoke several times and heard blue geese flying southward. The next day, when the air was filled with snow, more flocks flew over. Some were in V formations, some in straight lines, and others were in mixed, straggling bands. Our mode of travel seemed mere plodding when I watched those geese speeding along. I thought of the year before, when I had stood on the banks of Moose River and watched those travelers starting joyously for the south, while I remained to face a subarctic winter. This time I too was going south, and the thought gave me a feeling of companionship with those mighty travelers of the sky.

A few days later, when I was again walking the board sidewalks of Cochrane, Ontario, eating my meals at a hotel, my months in Hudson Bay seemed already a dream. That land seemed far away.

It was not the winter storms sweeping down across the ice that I thought of now, nor the sea-sickness on the little rolling steamer. My memory went back to Nastapoka in June, when seals lay on floating ice pans in the sun; to the snow bunting singing sweetly from his perch on a boulder; and the charming little meadows, abloom with Arctic flowers.

The Labrador Peninsula

Two years later I was once more going north, into the unknown, this time farther east. That persistent ornithologist, Mr. Todd, wanted to learn what birds lived in interior Labrador, and I was again privileged to go with him. We were to enhance the collections and the knowledge residing in Carnegie Museum in Pittsburgh.

This time it was a bigger expedition. We had three nineteen-foot Peterborough freight canoes, all well loaded, and five Indians. Mr. Todd was, of course, to lead the expedition; I was to be his assistant, collecting specimens and taking scientific notes. The third white man of our party was Mr. Alfred Marshall, a retired businessman of Chicago who was paying half the expense of the trip in order to fish and enjoy wild country. He was an athletic, cheerful person, enjoying to the full the superb fishing he found all across Labrador. And he joyfully helped us collect certain specimens also.

There were three big canoes and the five experienced Indians. But it takes two to handle a canoe—one in the bow and one in the stern. Since I was the youngest of the party, I became the sixth Indian, much to my satisfaction.

We did have some language barriers. Three of the Indians were tall and vigorous Ojibways, who spoke their own tongue, French, and English. The tallest one was named Mose Odjik; the other two, Jocko and Paul Commanda, had been with us two years before on Hudson Bay. Then there were two Cree Indians of Labrador, Charles and Philip, who knew something about the country we were entering. They were slighter in build, but how they could handle a canoe! They spoke French, but very little English. They would speak French to the Ojibways, who in turn spoke English to us—and thus we managed!

On May 26, 1917, we started up the Ste. Marguerite River from our camp near Clarke City, in the St. Lawrence gulf region. Our destination was away up north—across Labrador to Hudson Strait. Paul Commanda, the veteran canoe guide, was in the bow of one canoe and Mose Odjik in the stern, with Todd and Marshall in the middle. It was fitting that Charles and Philip, who both knew Cree and French, should have one canoe together. So Jocko was in the stern of the third canoe, with me as his bowsman. How would we do, with all the languages and personalities involved?

This time we were faced with going upstream much of the time, and had to use poles instead of paddles. Day after day, headed for the unknown interior of Labrador, we labored along with poles against the current. I, of course, became intimate with Jocko, who was teaching me so much about handling our canoe.

We had not gone many days on our way when it was brought forcibly to me how important little things can be in the wilderness. It was a very swift river we were going up; naturally, we were going along close to shore, both of us standing. Farther out, the river was too deep for our poles. Jocko in the stern would shove the canoe forward, the bow tending to turn toward shore as he shoved. I, in the bow, also pushed forward, but my effort shoved the bow out. Thus we corrected each other as we went along.

Ahead of us I saw a huge rock a little way out from the bank. The water rushing by on the outside was too deep, and between the rock and the bank the water came boiling through at a steeply slanting, fast pace. We headed up into this fast water near shore.

Halfway through, I was as usual pushing the bow away from shore. Suddenly an urgent command came from the stern: "Shove in to shore, *Bateese!*" (The Indians had nicknamed me "Baptiste".)

I suddenly realized that the rock prevented Jocko from shoving the stern out to correct my shove. We could have gone crosswise to the rock, and the canoe and all its contents would have been dumped over in the swift current. But we made it, thanks to Jocko's quick command. And thus, each day, the youngest member of the party was learning!

We all helped each other as we went along. Mr. Todd and I were of course responsible for collecting specimens. Each night I put out some mouse traps to gather information on the extent of small mammal species across Labrador. But everyone in the party got specimens of birds and helped in every way they could. Marshall was happy to help in this way when he wasn't busy fishing.

Once, later in the season, when geese were flightless, we captured a goose out on a lake. I had with me some aluminum bands. When I had banded the bird and turned it loose, Charles cried out in a surprised voice, "No!" He could not understand anyone turning loose a captured bird.

Paul was the cook, but all the Indians helped in setting up camp each night, building a fire, and attending to other camp chores. They had full control of the canoes, afloat or ashore. While they were doing all these things, I would put out my traps. Marshall often went fishing and we had all the fish we needed in camp. While all this was going on, Mr. Todd was taking care of specimens and writing detailed notes.

So it went, day after day, as we traveled into the heart of Labrador. I cannot begin to tell of all our little adventures, but a few stand out in memory. I was impressed with the song of the winter wren—trilling, happy music. It was so lively that I attempted to write it, somehow, in my journal:

rrrrr	se	se	serrrrrrr		sie
[trill]	se	se	se	[trill]	rrrr sie
					[low]

Jocko was teaching me some Ojibway words, but it took me days to learn his word for this tiny winter wren. Finally I got it written down to his satisfaction: *Ka-wi-miti-go-zhi-que-na-ga-mooch.* Such a long name for a tiny bird! He said the name meant "little French woman singer." This Indian name is surely evidence of the white man's influence.

Jocko and I became intimate enough that we could kid each other. As we poled along, he would say to me: "*Kawin nishishin shogenosh!* ('No good white man!')." To show off my meager knowledge of his language, I would reply, "*Kawin nishishin ishenabe!* ('No good Indian!')." And so we got along fine.

One day, on a slope high above us, we saw a black bear followed by a cub. We watched them crossing through an open place into trees beyond. A black bear is a common sight for many people today along certain roads, but I shall never forget that view from a canoe, up there in primitive, seldom-visited surroundings. Also, it was the first bear I had seen, and the only one I saw on that trip.

On another day, while we were resting on a portage, other inhabitants of this northern wilderness came into view. An Indian came walking along the portage, carrying a canoe. Behind him came his wife with a big pack on her back, and on top of the pack a small child. They stopped to pass the time of day with our two Cree Indians. While the woman stood there, not saying much, her child suddenly tumbled off the pack to the ground. Calmly the mother picked the youngster up and tossed him back onto the pack as though he were just another piece of dunnage. Presently they both went on, headed the way we had come.

These were the only human beings we met until we reached northern Labrador later in the summer. But someone had been up here. One day we were struggling against a strong current past some large rocks. There, in a crack in one of the rocks, was a canoe paddle! What catastrophe had happened here in the rapids? We never knew.

No scientific expedition had been all the way across Labrador, seven hundred miles south to north. Ours was to be the first. Very few Indians had been across, but Philip knew some of the geography of the southern area. One evening, when we had studied again our incomplete map, we all suddenly agreed that we were not on the best route—that instead of going up the Ste. Marguerite River, we should have gone up the Moisie. Paul was disgruntled and a bit sarcastic; the other Indians were somber and didn't say much. Apparently we were on the wrong track. What should we do?

We finally decided to cross over to the Moisie River system. We found out how spotted with lakes, ponds, and streams interior Labrador is—and how big! With much poling, paddling, and portaging, while still in the Ste. Marguerite watershed, almost to its head, we finally made it over to the Moisie River headwaters on July 15.

Interior Labrador is substantially a high, irregular plateau, about 4,000 feet in elevation, dotted with lakes and forested low hills between the many streams. We also saw many burned-over areas—cause unknown. There were many rainy days all summer long.

I tried to express in my diary the effect this big country had upon me. On May 27 I wrote, "I came up on a ridge and stood still there a while. The wind was cold; there were patches of snow, down logs and brush heaps. At first sight an uninteresting place. All at once I found the place alive with birds. A ruby-crowned kinglet appeared, seeking among the balsam twigs. He came up close, showing his ruby crown and his bright white-ringed eye. At intervals he sang and I could see his throat vibrate, but meanwhile he kept on seeking industriously. Flit-flip he went, from twig to twig, glancing this way and that in his everlasting search. Once he reached up and picked a tiny morsel from a branch overhead. He made a little swoop out in the air, and I heard his beak snap as he caught a little insect, then went on to the next twig.

"Another one came along, his ruby crown gleaming. Hopping, seeking, he passed on into the distance.

"A downy woodpecker then lit on a small limb near me and I heard him scraping his way up over the tree's bark. He came up closer onto a small birch sapling. Here he tapped away as he hitched upward, stopping in one spot to peck quite a while. Suddenly he dropped to a dry limb below. He gave a sharp 'spik,' and kept on, craned his head and looked around once, then flew up to another dry limb. From there to another, and another, then suddenly dived down the hill to another dry sapling. The downy is a busy fellow, only taking time to give you a mere glance and perhaps an exclamatory 'spik,' and then goes on with his business.

"A winter wren was singing in the distance somewhere."

Common birds these, and well-known. But to me, up there in the Labrador northland, the occasion was unique. The place itself and the circumstances meant as much to me as the birds.

Thus we observed, recorded, and enjoyed the bird life through Labrador —thrushes, warblers, sparrows, flycatchers, grouse—so many kinds in this north country. Waterfowl were on the lakes, shorebirds along the borders, hawks overhead, and owls in the forest. We found a nest of the bald eagle, saw the kingfisher, and watched the nighthawk swooping in the evening sky.

It was surprising how well the Indians knew the lives of the birds. When Charles, Philip, and I went off to look for caribou, the day was made memorable for me by all the bird life we saw. We did not even see a caribou, but I was impressed by how carefully Philip examined tracks to see how recent they were. We came on one very clear track in the earth. "Loup!" Charles exclaimed. (He pronounced it "lo".) It was the only sign of a wolf we saw on that whole trip.

On this day we reached a point where the forest seemed to indicate the Hudsonian Life Zone. In the lower areas, we had been in the Canadian Life Zone. The forest intrigued me. I could not help wondering about life in various forms up here. On June 7, out from camp on a field day, I entered this soliloquy in my journal:

"Now all is still. The farther shore is dark and indistinct. Flecks of foam float silently along and the woods life goes on as it has for ages. The little dead tamarack by me must be at least 30 years old, and the birch sapling ten or fifteen—all that time they have stood in this spot. Winters have come and gone. Summer, rain, sunshine and wind, Indian hunters—all have passed here. Beavers have lived in the pond, birds have sung and nested here—it is wonderful to think of all that has happened in the lifetime of these trees, and in the ages before. Tonight it is growing dark once more—not a bird note now, only the steady droning of the rapid at the foot of the pond—a wonderful, peaceful place."

How did all this appeal to the others? I don't know, but it seems significant to me that one evening I found Marshall stooping at the side of a pond, feeding a frog, giving it flies and bits of meat. The frog was blind in one eye.

Again on June 17 I went up over the hills at dusk and was moved to try to express what I felt in the journal:

"There was a delicate purple sunset, tall dead trees silhouetted against it. As I came to the top, I had a view of the rolling hills, bare except for a grove of trees here and there in the distance. Clumps of wild cherry shrubs in bloom dotted the slopes, and bumblebees were still buzzing about among them. From a clump of spruce over against the sunset came the songs of olive-backed thrushes. Occasionally a white-throated sparrow piped up, while behind me, over the river, two nighthawks were swooping and calling. Labrador may be a barren, desolate land, but at moments like this there is the charm of nature at her best."

There were other such beautiful moments as we crossed Labrador. Then came a crisis, man-made. We were far into the wilderness but had not yet reached the height of land. The Indians now asked for a raise in wages—up to $95 a month. My interpretation of the situation was that we were in unknown, unmapped country, and the Indians were hesitant about going on. But I had nothing to do with it; the decision was up to our leader, Mr. Todd. Alfred Marshall, with his businessman's acumen, privately advised him that they were not really asking a great deal and that their demands should be met. This was done.

Then they came up with another objection: our outfit was too heavy. The upshot of this argument was that we left behind, in the middle of Labrador, one canoe, fully loaded! Each of us donated to the discard anything we thought we could get along without. But we kept all the food—bacon, beans, flour, dried fruit, and all the rest. One of these items bothered Mose Odjik and me—a case of condensed milk. It was heavy, and we thought of the many portages still lying ahead. We could surely get along without that milk!

I smiled at him and asked, "Mose, do you like milk?"

He smiled broadly and replied: "Yes, *Bateese*, I like it very much!" At every meal thereafter Mose and I were mixing and drinking milk, and in just a few days we had no case of milk to carry over the portages. No one said anything.

For a while I hardly knew where we were. We had to assume that the two Cree Indians knew what they were doing. At times we poled upstream, crossed a lake, then went downstream again. But we were going somewhere!

One day we saw a letter on a piece of birchbark, fastened to a tree. Charles went ashore and read it. An Indian mailman had gone through here and cached his gun and other supplies—a mailman in the center of Ungava! The Indians went everywhere, sooner or later.

At this time Marshall and I were traveling in the Cree Indian canoe. I remember so keenly going down the rapids—the great thrills of the trip. Charles called them *Oposh-kosh-kass*, which he said referred to the big swells. And they were big! We crossed over once—why I never knew—and at one point we were crosswise to the current. But Philip knew his job and swung to meet the swells. When Charles, in the bow, paddled hard, I paddled hard in the middle seat, too. Philip was tense with watchfulness, calling to Charles often and sharply about where to go. But at one point when we were going straight and smoothly for a few moments, Charles looked back at me, smiled, and said: "Hallo, *Bateese!*"

Finally we paddled into an eddy and landed at a portage. Only then did Philip smile. He had been very sober and earnest all through, but now he laughed, and we all relaxed after our tension.

One day our portage led us to a large lake. While we made camp, the Indians went up the shore to look for the portage out. Toward evening they came back to camp looking glum. No portage! It was a gloomy, somber group around the campfire that night. What next?

Next morning I went up along the lake, seeing many birds and collecting some specimens. I tramped on for a long time, and near the end of the lake I suddenly saw a cached canoe and several snowshoes. Here was the portage! The Indians had been out but had not gone far enough.

When I got back to camp, the atmosphere was still gloomy. What a difference when I told them of my find! What laughter and chatter around our campfire that night! Next morning we were on our way again, in high spirits.

On August 4 we portaged, crossed a series of little lakes one after another, and when we came to still another lake, we found the outlet flowing northward! We had crossed the height of land, in the interior of the Labrador peninsula. From here on, our poling was over; we were going downstream toward Fort Chimo, still far away. It would not be all river travel; of course, there were still a lot of lakes to paddle across.

I was confused by this height-of-land country. Streams and rivers seemed to be going in so many directions, and up to this point we had been going in several directions ourselves! But apparently we were on the way. One day we came to old Fort Nascaupie, near the height of land. It had been abandoned for some forty years, yet in the clearing about the old remains fireweed and rhubarb were growing. We also found part of an old cabin and some iron stoves—little signs of an earlier bit of civilization. And we ate rhubarb sauce that night!

One day soon after this we were going down a wide stream at a rapid rate. Through the clear water I could see the rocks and pebbles on the bottom flying past our canoe so rapidly that it scared me. I began to wonder—and just then we heard the roar of a waterfall ahead of us! Instantly the canoes were headed for shore, everyone paddling with all his strength. We barely made it. Just ahead was a huge waterfall plunging into a deep, vertical-walled canyon!

After gazing in awe at what we had barely escaped, we cautiously, with a hard struggle, made our way back up the swift current into the lake. We found no portage but eventually found our way by portaging over some high country and down to where the same stream was navigable again.

This was a region of waterfalls. A few days later we had an experience of a different kind. We had made our camp just above a waterfall of perhaps thirty feet in vertical drop. In the stream above the falls was a family of harlequin ducks, a mother and a brood of downy young. Always on the lookout for pictures, I got out my camera and went after them. As I approached, the female flew out over the falls, complaining. The river was too swift toward the center, and the little ones kept close to shore. I slowly crowded them, until they pattered up past me as far out as they dared. I did this several times in order to get some pictures, while the mother kept flying up and down over the falls, complaining.

Then, as I was crowding them for one last picture, Marshall appeared, coming along the shore toward me. This time the ducklings went out too far, and all of them were swept down over the brink, some thirty feet, to the turmoil below. I felt conscience-stricken—a whole brood of these beautiful ducks sacrificed for a picture! Once more the mother duck flew down over the falls.

Marshall and I rushed over to look down. There, below the white spume and turbulence, where waves were smoothing out, those downy young ducks were swimming downstream, shaking their down to get rid of the wetness. They had done something human beings could never have done.

Now for a time it seemed as though we were constantly portaging, running rapids, or paddling against a wind. One day Charles and Philip took Marshall and me along when they ran a rapid. As always, it was a great thrill. When we went ashore in the quiet water below, Marshall took out two five-dollar gold pieces and handed one to each of the Indians, remarking, "I like to see a man who knows his business!"

Big, tall Mose and I had become very friendly. I think it was he who nicknamed me "*Bateese*." One day he gave me a surprise. We had come to one of the many rapids, and as usual the Indians all looked it over to see if it were passable. They decided to portage around. When we stopped for lunch on the portage, one empty canoe still remained at the head of the rapids. As we sat there eating, Mose remarked: "*Bateese* and I will run that canoe down. I think we make it with empty canoe."

I was astounded. I had never steered a canoe down a rapids. But with

Mose in the stern to do the main steering, I was sure we could make it, and I began to look forward to it. After lunch Mose and I went back to the canoe. I picked up my paddle and started to climb in to go to the bow. But Mose, with the other paddle, at once climbed to the bow and shoved off!

I could do nothing about it; we were off, and I quickly sat down. Here was I, in the strategic place in the canoe, starting down a difficult rapids. Ahead of me I could see only a sea of big waves, and I had no idea where to go. And we were tearing along.

Then Mose said, "Look out dat rock, *Bateese!*"

I looked hard to see a rock somewhere ahead. Then he said again in a raised voice, urgently, "Look out dat rock, *Bateese!*"

I looked harder than ever, frantically, but could see nothing but waves. We were going so fast! Then Mose said, "That's the way to do it, *Bateese!*"

I don't know how, but we made it down that fast, tumbling water. Later, when Mose bragged to the other Indians about my ability, I felt guilty, but I kept still. I had never seen that rock!

When this trip was first planned, back on the St. Lawrence, Marshall and I were officially advised to keep shaved regularly—so we grew beards all summer! On August 14 I shaved for the first time, and a few days later Marshall gave in and took off his luxuriant growth.

I have neglected to mention the mosquitoes and black flies. Never have I seen them more numerous anywhere in the north. I think the less said about them, the better. We wore headnets.

On August 18 we came to a large Indian encampment and stayed the night there. The Indians knew the route to Fort Chimo, and we decided to hire two of them as guides to facilitate our travel and obviate all guesswork. We would soon be on the Koksoak River and near the end of our canoe journey. So we gave the two new Indians a supply of food to last them all the way down.

That night the Indian village had a feast! Next night, when we made camp down the river, I noticed that those two Indians set a net for trout; they lived on fish only for the rest of the trip! Their overturned canoe was their shelter, and I could see only one blanket.

As I have said, we had mosquitoes, but they and the other obstacles we encountered did not prevent us from enjoying what we saw. We were still on the Kaniapiskau River, a tributary of the Koksoak, and I find in my journal for August 19:

"It was raining today—sunshine and showers—and I saw the most brilliant rainbow I have ever seen. Two faint rainbows extended off across the water in different directions; a third appeared in the sky to the left. As we came up toward a rocky point, one of those on the water extended up and arched the sky, taking on the deepest and most perfect colors I have seen in a rainbow. The Indian canoe drifted in then, just where the rainbow touched the water.

"We rounded the point and there was a wonderful picture—the wild, rocky cliff towering above us, the rainbow arching out from behind it, sweeping down to the water, and behind it all, the grand river flowing on into rocky hills and bluffs. The wind was blowing us on in gusts; the rain was just letting up—a wild, beautiful moment, a mixture of grandeur and colorful beauty."

Didn't the wildness of our environment, which we could not analyze, enhance the scene we saw?

On August 22 we finally arrived at the Hudson's Bay Company trading post at Fort Chimo. As we climbed ashore and went up toward the buildings, the people there—Mr. Watt, the trader, and several others—came to greet us. As we came into the warm building, we saw a banner that read, "Welcome to Chimo!"

This was the end of our long summer's trip across the Labrador peninsula. The St. Lawrence now seemed far away to the south. We had a great mass of specimens and voluminous notes on the animal life of this land.

Two things we learned at Chimo: An Indian mailman coming all the way from Seven Islands down on the St. Lawrence arrived a few days after us. We were not the only ones! And the S.S. *Nascaupie* had not yet arrived on her way back out to "civilization." So we had plenty of time to collect more specimens here on the lower Koksoak River. We found many gyrfalcons and other falcons, hawks, snowy owls, and other Arctic species. At Fort Chimo we had reached the end of forest growth. To the south we could see the forest, and to the north barren landscape. The last trees were the tamaracks.

Now we were in true lemming country, and this was a year of high lemming population. I got all the specimens I wanted without trapping, merely by digging out their mossy burrows and seizing them by hand. On September 19, near the mouth of the Koksoak, I had an interesting observation of a lemming. From my journal: "Down near the water one of these mice was trying to get into a burrow. When I approached, I saw his hole was full of water. The mouse dived in, trying to work down into the burrow, then came out for air. When I touched it, down it went again, until at last it became angry and ground its teeth, refusing to go down again. Finally, it came out and ran off among the rocks."

About this time the autumn colors were coming over the landscape, coloring the tamarack forest. I was north of the tree limit when I wrote:

"The slopes are beautiful now, rich in autumn colors in spite of the absence of trees. Among the jagged, broken rocks lie little patches, meadows, and slopes of moss, with clumps of willows in autumn yellow, smaller shrubs in various browns, and others in flaming red. Today the distant landscape was a wonderful purple-blue."

Again on September 29: "The tamaracks are all old gold now, while the rocks are patched with clumps of red, yellow, and various browns, with gray and white boulders here and there. The autumn is beautiful."

But pleasant as it might be, it had to end. Our ship arrived, and we remained for a few days at the trading post packing our specimens and all our gear for the trip on the steamer. Our camping—weeks and weeks of it—was over.

We said our good-byes to all the good, helpful people at the post and started on our southward voyage October 6. The Far North had said good-bye to us the night before with a display of the aurora.

Our trip down the Labrador coast was made more interesting by the presence on board of a priest-missionary from Baffin Island, who told us interesting tales of that country. He said that when a caribou was killed in winter, its hide was frozen. But if there was no wood or seal oil for a fire, an Eskimo woman would put the hide around her body, next to her skin, to thaw it so it could be cleaned. And at times, women would put a bag of snow behind and one in front, next to their bodies, to melt the snow into water. Could I believe all this? He was a priest!

After a few days we were in rougher seas, and I was seasick. Reaching St. John's was a great relief, but there was regret, too, for here we said good-bye to Alfred Marshall, who boarded a train there. He had been a fine companion all the way.

And at Montreal on October 23, Mr. Todd and I said our good-byes to those wonderful Indians. They were back in their home territory now, and the trip was really ended. But fond memories have lived on through the years.

Harold Udgarden, a "servant" for the Hudson's Bay Company at Great Whale River, with his Eskimo wife.

Eskimo women sewing a sealskin kayak cover, along the Nastapoka River.

An Indian lodge housing several families, east coast of Hudson Bay.

Canoeing on a Labrador stream.

*Cree Indian with native stone pipe, Great Whale
River, 1915.*

Olaus banding a guillemot, east coast of Hudson Bay.

Olaus and his brother Adolph, photographed by their Eskimo friend Pooto high in the Brooks Range of Alaska.

ALASKA: THE EARLY YEARS

In Search of the Caribou

In 1920 I had been given a job with the United States Biological Survey. The veteran naturalist Dr. Edward W. Nelson was its chief. He had been in Alaska as early as 1877 and was interested in learning the habits and migrations of caribou in Alaska and Yukon Territory. I felt honored to be given this assignment, and it was stimulating to work under the supervision of a man like Dr. Nelson. But what an assignment—to find out all I could about caribou in this whole immense region of the North!

On March 22, 1921, I had left Fairbanks with dogteam to go up the Tanana River and other places to study this northern deer. That was before the day of airplanes, and everybody traveled with dogs. It was a snowy day—not an auspicious start for a long trip. I planned to spend the first night at the Eighteen-Mile Roadhouse, but when I reached the roadhouse that evening, I found the door padlocked. The place had been advertised as a roadhouse, and at that time cabins on the frontier were not locked. I mention this here because it was the only time I ever broke into a house! I hesitated a while, then pulled the staples, went in, and made myself at home. I hoped that when the owner came home, he would understand that I was a traveler needing a night's shelter and meant no harm.

Well, he came and at first looked disgruntled—someone had broken into his home! Without saying much he prepared supper and after a while we were discussing game and other woodsy subjects like two old buddies. So I spent a good night in a roadhouse after all.

I made my way up to Tanana Crossing, an Indian village and mission (now called Tanacross). From there I went across to Eagle on the upper Yukon River, not arriving until the middle of April. Along the way I interviewed prospectors and Indians, as to where and when they had seen caribou, and I gathered a lot of valuable data on caribou migration.

Whenever I started off on a trip, I notified my superiors in Washington. I had done so this time too, but it proved to be a long trip far from any settlements, with no way to get word out again. My chief, Dr. Nelson, who had been in Alaska and had kept in close touch with my work, became worried when he did not hear from me for so many weeks. He telegraphed the United States marshal in Fairbanks that he would furnish the money to send out a search party for me. When I arrived at Eagle, where there was a US Signal Corps station, and sent a wire to Washington, the excitement subsided.

I traveled back to Tanana Crossing to observe the spring migration of caribou. There I became acquainted with Tom Yeigh, a real woodsman. As a result of our conversations, we decided to go up the Robertson River after the "breakup." We needed a boat, which was no problem for resourceful Tom. Somehow he managed to ripsaw a pile of boards from nearby spruce trees, and with these we built a poling boat.

On May 25 we started down the Tanana River in our new poling boat, leaving my dogs to be cared for by some Indians at the village until our return.

This proved to be one of the outstanding trips of my Alaskan fieldwork. We drifted easily down to the mouth of the Robertson River, where our heavy work began, for we had to pole up that swift stream. There near the mouth of the river, we came upon a phenomenon common throughout the north country of our planet—the overflow ice. In Siberia they call it *aufeis*. In the winter, when ice becomes very thick, the pressure underneath is so great at some places on a stream that water breaks through and overflows the ice. That freezes, then the water breaks through again and freezes again.

This is repeated until the overflow ice is an average of three or four feet thick. Here on the Robertson we found ice close to six feet thick. In spring the streams flow through, open and normal, but sometimes it takes most of the summer for the ice on the flats at the sides of the streams to thaw away.

Most of the time we poled against the current, but sometimes we had to pull it. Attaching a long rope to the boat's bow, with a bridle to keep the bow out in the current, one of us would walk along the bank and pull while the other stayed in the boat to keep it off the shore. For several days we would struggle against the current. Eventually we found ourselves in the mountains of the Alaska Range and there set up a permanent camp. We figured that from that point we could explore the country and learn what was living in it.

I thought back to the time earlier that season, when I had observed the spring migration of caribou coming over these mountains all the way from the Copper River country where they had spent the winter. What a sight it had been to watch herds of these animals coming down the snowy mountainsides into the Tanana Valley. They were headed for the fawning grounds of the Yukon-Tanana uplands.

"The freshness, the freedom, the farness . . . " I could not help thinking that these attributes so well expressed by the poet Robert Service are inherent in caribou nature. Those animals, with only themselves to rely on, could cross the huge snowy Alaska Range, into the far interior of Alaska. Other creatures, too, had the same instinct. Flock after flock of sandhill cranes had come flying overhead that spring, coming from far to the south where they had spent the winter, headed for the wetlands of the Arctic tundra where they would have their nests and spend the summer. Inspiring events in the natural world!

As we traveled on foot along the river bars and on the mountainsides of the Robertson River country, we found many fascinating evidences of the rich life of the north. There were still a few caribou lingering here, and it was mountain sheep country, too. One day I climbed high up among the cliffs and collected an old ram. We needed meat, and I wanted to get a good museum specimen. The ram made an excellent specimen. I could tell by the great sweeping horns and the annual growth rings that he was close to fourteen years old, about the age limit for mountain sheep. Usually mountain sheep is the choicest of all wild game in the north, but this animal had just come through a hard winter, and the meat was so stringy and tough we could hardly eat it. In exasperation Tom exclaimed: "I never saw meat so tough I couldn't cook it!"

There was so much life up here! We saw many porcupines. They chew on old, shed antlers and gnaw many kinds of things. One came right up to me one day and sniffed at my shoe, looked up, sniffed again, and finally wandered off. One time I watched one of them nibbling some mud on a river bar; his nose must have indicated a chemical element he wanted.

One of my objectives in coming up the Robertson was to obtain bears for the museum. I had been told this was a good place, and the bears in the upper Tanana valley offered a puzzling biological phenomenon as well.

Along the Tanana and tributaries many of the grizzlies were of a light color. Local people referred to them as "glacier bears" (not to be confused with the color phase of the black bear of the southern coastal regions of Alaska which is called "glacier bear"). We saw several grizzlies of this light color phase in the distance, and later in our trip I collected one which was almost pure white.

Early on our trip up the river Tom got a black bear. In shooting it, he gave me a shock that I still remember. At the first shot the bear was only wounded, and the pain caused him to writhe and give out an agonized wail, so human in quality that it aroused in me a sympathetic feeling that I never forgot. With another shot Tom quickly put the animal out of its misery. Since then I have learned that an injured black bear will always give vent to his feelings in this manner.

One of the outstanding events of our trip occurred one day on the Robertson. That morning Tom and I decided to go upriver and try for another grizzly specimen. We put a light lunch in our packsacks and, with our rifles, started upriver.

We had had our lunch and started off again when we saw our specimen, a large brown grizzly, coming down the valley. He was across the river, approaching along the opposite bank. With our rifles ready, we settled down and waited.

"Tom, let's each aim and fire when ready, without waiting for the other. What do you think?"

"Yep, that's fine."

The bear came onto the open bar directly opposite us, and we both fired two or three shots at intervals. He ran a few yards, as grizzlies usually do when wounded, then dropped. We didn't know whether one or both of us had hit him, but we had our specimen.

Only then did we realize our predicament: the river here was too deep to ford. I did want that specimen and did not want an animal to go to waste. We discussed the problem and finally agreed to do something drastic—to go up to the head of the river at its glacier in the mountains, come down the other side to our bear, and continue down to a point opposite camp. There we knew the river split up into several ribbon-like channels, and we assumed we could ford it. So we shouldered our packs and started on up.

It turned out to be a longer trip than we had anticipated. We tramped on, hour after hour, and it was one o'clock in the morning when we reached the bear! But we had cast our die, and there was nothing else to do. I carefully measured the bear, and we skinned it. By this time we were so tired we lay down on the bar, and for about an hour we dozed. Then it began to sprinkle, so we bundled the hide and the skull into our packs and went on downriver.

It was about eight o'clock in the morning before we got down opposite our camp. We had been out about twenty-four hours, and camp looked good across there. We had long before stopped and eaten the few bits of food left from our lunches.

At this moment I happened to look up into the mountains, and there I saw a flock of white mountain sheep. Our camp larder was getting low, and we were depending more and more on flour and rice. I got a sudden urge.

"Tom, if you'll take this bear specimen across to camp, I'd like to go up there and get a young sheep for camp meat."

"My gosh, you're not goin' back up in those mountains now, are yuh?"

"Yes, I might as well as long as I'm on this side of the river. Besides it doesn't look very far, and it seems to be nice, green, open country."

Tom looked skeptical, but he said, "All right, I'll take care of this specimen."

So off I went. My route lay up another branch of the Robertson. It was farther than I had thought—of course!—and I found obstacles in my way. Tom had been right to be skeptical about my notion. The sheep that had looked so close were really on the top of a high mountain and what looked like a smooth, green slope in the distance turned out to be made up of alder bushes, all slanting downhill to impede my progress. I don't know how so much time could pass. I was traveling right along as efficiently as I could, but when I finally got up near the sheep, it was past midnight again! Of course, I should mention that we were in the north country where we had "midnight light" if not actually the midnight sun; it was full light all the time.

Apparently those sheep were not used to seeing human beings. They looked at me as I approached them, and continued to lie there. I felt a pang of guilt for intruding on their domestic peace. But man wants meat to eat, and I had come up here for that purpose. I thought one of two yearlings near me would be suitable, and I shot him. At the report of the gun, most of the flock arose, and some ran off a little way. But I was amazed to see that the other yearling, lying there beside the dead one, did not even get up. I walked up to within a few yards of a ewe nearby and we stood there looking at each other. Apparently these animals were not familiar with gunshot either. Surely here was nature's unspoiled domain.

Eventually the sheep moved off a bit; I dressed out the yearling, prepared it for camp use, put all the meat into my pack, and started my descent.

My habit of stopping occasionally to look around and contemplate things did take some time. At one place a white-tailed ptarmigan flew off a ridge into space. As I saw him, I looked across this part of the earth at the ridges and cliffs, at peak after peak, far off to where clouds of fog were drifting. The ptarmigan had chosen this high country to live in, higher than that chosen by the other two species of ptarmigan. And those mountain sheep over there—they, too, had chosen the high cliffs as their home. I was filled with wonder.

I did not get back to camp until about four-thirty that morning. I had been gone nearly two days and nights with just a taste of food and hardly any sleep. I crawled into bed and slept around the clock. Neither Tom nor I felt any ill effects, and we had a fine grizzly specimen and plenty of camp meat.

The time came to leave the Robertson, but we had seen much of the wildlife living in that valley, and I had the specimens of bears that I needed. So, with all supplies and specimens packed in the boat, we started down the river on June 19. We had struggled for three days to get up to this place. We went back down in two hours.

On the Tanana River we found high water, endured rainy days, and had rather a hard time of it. But we were not the only ones who had trouble. On the way down in May, there had been a number of geese nesting on the river bars. Now this unusual high water had flooded their nests, and they were flying about us in dismay, not knowing where to go.

At midnight June 25, after a long hard day of poling, we arrived at Tanana Crossing. We had enjoyed a rich experience on the Robertson. I never dreamed that thirty-seven years later I would be gazing down on that same dramatic country from an airplane.

Tom Yeigh and I planned another trip, this time east of Tanana Crossing into the Ketchumstuk country, a big caribou migration route and part of their fawning ground. It was summer, but we could not depend on river travel in the region we wanted to visit; the route was all overland, and we would have to go on foot. Tom, as eager as I to go places, no matter what the obstacles, suggested, "Well, we could pack some of our dogs and carry packs ourselves."

"The trouble is, I have to carry a lot of taxidermy material and photography stuff, and I would like to take along some sketching and painting material, too," I said.

"I don't want to pack more than seventeen pounds per dog, and I want to take along some simple spring scales to make sure," he insisted. He was very particular not to pack his dogs too heavily. "But we can depend on fish here and there, to feed the dogs."

Later I learned that the Indians would sometimes pack as much as fifty pounds on a dog, and I appreciated Tom's consideration for his animals. The Indians helped me to make dog packs, with two panniers of canvas, patterned after the moose or caribou skin ones of earlier Indians.

Finally we had our gear ready. Tom suggested that we travel lighter by not taking a tent or blankets. I had never done that, but I agreed. If Tom could do it, surely I could, too. He had two dogs to pack, and I took two of mine, and on July 2 we started off—two men and four dogs, each with a pack.

This was a new way of life for me, and new for my dogs, too. Jack and Black Tom had been my companions on many winter trips, and we knew each other well. When I put the pack on Jack, he turned around and looked surprised. What was this on his back? But as the days went on he got used to it.

When bedtime came that evening, I put on my headnet to frustrate the mosquitoes, with a towel over my head to hold the net away from my face. Then, tucking my hands up the opposite sleeves of my jacket, I curled up on the ground near the fire just as Tom and the dogs did, and we all went to sleep for the night, although it was always daylight.

After a few days' travel we came to a small Indian village and learned much about the caribou by talking with those people. We also met Dick Mitchell, a white man who was raising hay in a meadow there, and to my surprise, also had a few horses, though this was neither horse country nor farming country.

This was very wet land, and we often had to wade in water; sometimes it was difficult to find a place dry enough for a camp. However, we saw bands of caribou and learned much about their travels by talking with the Indians we met and the few white men who had spent many years in this part of Alaska.

We also came upon something which stirred our imaginations, something from Indian life far back in history—the Indian-made caribou snare fences. I had seen some short fragments elsewhere, but in this Ketchumstuk country, the heart of the caribou migration routes, the snare fences were most extensive and sophisticated. These fences and the lookout trees illustrated very well how early human inhabitants here lived with the caribou, both of them having inherited this primeval environment.

One snare we saw was near the head of Little Dennison River. It was about a mile long and consisted of a fence made of four or five rails, varying in different parts to a height of four or five feet. The Indians had no nails or wire, so these rails were fastened with willow withes, cleverly twisted to hold them in place. At intervals there would be a gap in the fence, in which a snare had been suspended. In earlier times these snares were made of caribou rawhide. I have one such snare from Old Crow Village in Yukon Territory. Here in the Ketchumstuk country the Indians had taken advantage of the white man's material. In the first years of this century, the United States government had built a telegraph line through this part of Alaska, from Valdez to Eagle, and also from Eagle to Nome via Tanana. This line, later abandoned, left many miles of wire lying across the interior country, and the Indians used it to make caribou snares. In one such gap in the fence lay the skeleton of a caribou, the closed snare still around the cervical vertebrae. Evidently this had been an abandoned caribou, found too late to use. I also found a lookout tree, with a platform fastened high up the trunk, where one could watch for caribou approaching in the distance.

Dick Mitchell took me out to show me another version of the Indians' ingenuity. They had constructed a long snare fence extending six miles westward to Indian Creek, which also served as a drift fence. At one end of the fence was a pole corral 510 feet long into which the caribou were detoured. It had an opening about 30 feet wide at one end, to admit the animals, and a pocket at the other end where the killing took place. Later I asked an Indian how they handled the caribou once they were in the pocket. "Oh, we fastened a knife to the end of a pole and speared them through the fence."

In some parts of Alaska, moose also were snared in this way. In fact, just before my arrival at Tanana Crossing in early April, a young moose had been snared by the Indians near there. All of these methods were relics of the time before the invention of gunpowder, when the early inhabitants of Alaska lived by ingenuity and intimate knowledge of the habits of animals.

This abandoned wire of the white man, although a boon to the Indians who used it for snares, proved to be a special hazard to caribou. I found several places where a passing bull caribou had got tangled in the wire. The more he fought to get rid of it, the more wire wound about his antlers, until he finally reached the tree to which the wire was snubbed. There he hung, tethered to the tree, and died. I discovered such a skeleton, unwound the wire, and found that fifty-five feet of it had become wound about the antlers.

From Ketchumstuk we wandered on with our pack dogs over the caribou country, our camp life extremely simple. We "siwashed out" at night, lying by our fire as I suppose those Indians who built the fences had done. Everywhere we saw birds of all kinds, and my journal was filled with ornithological data about different kinds of sparrows, thrushes, yellowlegs, warblers, hawks, and owls. Up above timberline we saw such species as the wheatear—true Arctic birds.

One day I was fortunate in coming upon something that was scientifically precious. On a mountain slope above tree limit was a pair of surfbirds with some downy young ones. The surfbirds were known as a common wintering bird along the Pacific coast, and we knew they must go somewhere up north to nest, but no one had known where. Here was the first nesting record of the surfbird known to science.

I took one of the downy young and one adult as specimens, and they are now in the National Museum. In later years surfbirds were found nesting in the mountains of Mount McKinley National Park, again far above timberline.

We had depended on fishing to feed our dogs, but had no luck. We got a grouse or two, but that was meager food for four dogs. Finally we became desperate. As much as we hated to do it, we decided to kill a moose. There were plenty of them in this country, and we had to hunt only a short time. Tom did the shooting. We fed the dogs well and dried as much of the meat as we could possibly take along in our packs. Much of the moose still had to be wasted, but we felt we had no choice this time. We had seen a wolf track nearby, and I found myself hoping that the wolf, or a fox or wolverine, would find what remained of the moose.

A few days later we had a different kind of moose adventure. We came out of a stream bottom and were going up an open slope in bare country above the trees. Suddenly a moose appeared above us, running a slanting course across the hills. Things began to happen. My dogs were young and eager for a chase and sprang forward immediately. I yelled at them to come back. Jack, the big gray one, turned, looked at me, and hesitated. "Jack, Tom, come back here!" I yelled.

Then Jack looked at the fleeing moose and at Black Tom, who had not even looked back, and he joined the chase. All three animals disappeared over the hill and were gone. Tom's dogs were older and better trained, and they stayed with us. We couldn't very well go after the speeding animals—they were going too fast. "Better stay here for a while and see what happens," Tom suggested, and I could think of nothing better to do. So we sat there and waited, impatiently.

An hour passed. Suddenly Jack appeared over the hilltop. He still had his pack on, for which we were thankful. As he came up close, he swung his head low and acted very guilty. Although he had almost come back when I called him, I wanted to have him fully understand that he had done wrong. I gave him a light whipping, and he was content to lie down close to me. Black Tom was out there somewhere. Again we waited. We began to recount what he had in his pack, things we might lose—the skinning outfit, some specimens, a can of lard for cooking, and other things. Tom kept thinking about the lard; I thought of the specimens I had worked so hard to collect and prepare. Our tempers were not very sweet. We grumbled and mumbled—and waited.

Finally, after quite a long time, there appeared a black dog in the distance. I looked with my field glasses. He had no pack. When he came up he also acted guilty; he knew he had disobeyed. So I firmly administered discipline to him, too. We knew now what we had to do. We dreaded trying to follow dog tracks on that hard ground, but the moose hooves should have made some impression. So Tom and I shouldered our packs and began to follow the moose trail. We had no way of knowing how far we would have to go, but we had to recover that pack if possible.

It was still before noon. We found that we could follow the moose by an occasional track, over the hill, down across a flat, and on. Then we lost all traces and didn't know where to go next. It was about noon, so we thought we might as well have a bite of lunch and rest a bit. We were a glum pair as we sat there and worried.

After lunch we made a circle and found moose tracks again. So we continued on, finding an occasional track to keep on course. "Dog track!" I would call as I crossed a wet place.

"Here's the moose track," my partner would call, and I would edge over in his direction. We went on like this laboriously, for hours. Suddenly we saw the canvas pack cover before us. We went on carefully and eagerly. Soon we picked up a can of mammal skulls. A little farther, Tom called out in a matter-of-fact tone: "Here it is."

Our search was over. We had spent most of a day to recover materials lost because of my dogs' disobedience, but now we had everything and could go on.

As a postscript on the behavior of my dogs, I might say that I made a trip later that fall east of Fairbanks with the same two dogs packed. One day we came over a rise and surprised a herd of caribou, which all ran off. "Here!" I said to the dogs, and they stayed. They had learned.

Eventually, sleeping on the ground at night without bed or tent made me a little weary. The dogs were used to it, and Tom, the veteran woodsman, didn't say much about it. One day we came to a camp where someone had been with horses and had left some tattered pieces of horse blankets. I noticed that Tom was as eager as I that night to wrap a few pieces of the old horse blankets around us, a suggestion of a bed anyway.

After over two weeks of traveling about in this caribou country, seeing all kinds of wildlife, and gathering a volume of notes on caribou distribution and habits, we came back to Tanana Crossing. We had spent a couple of nights in a bed at Ketchumstuk, and again on July 15 at Dick Mitchell's place. But otherwise we had traveled as the early Indians did in summer. Alaska is not canoe or horse country. When I wanted to go anywhere in the hills in summer, I went on foot. The Indians showed me how to pack dogs, so I managed to get around. I had learned much in Ketchumstuk country, not only about the ecology of the animal life, but also through my association with the Indians and with Tom Yeigh, that real outdoorsman.

With Dogs Around Denali

You can see a dogteam is approaching, but the day is so cold that the team is enveloped in a cloud of vapor, and the dogs seem blurred. When they come closer, you see that the dogs are frosted with rime and the driver's parka and cap are white. Your own dogs, too, are rimed with frost.

These are some of the memories of frontier Alaska in the dog mushing days, before the automobile and airplane. There was struggle, of course—hard, wintry days of deep cold, minus forty, fifty, sixty, or more degrees.

Why do we look back to those days as something precious? Perhaps there was something there we do not yet understand. On those long dog trails, leading through miles of scrubby spruce forest, across lowland flats, over rolling hills, every traveler I met was a friend. We would maneuver our respective dogteams past each other in the narrow trail, plant a foot on the brake, and talk.

"How's the trail?"

"Pretty fair. Got into an overflow back there on the Toklat; but nothing bad. You'll have no trouble. Good-looking lead dog you've got there."

"Yeah, he's all right in a trail. A little footsore today. You come from Kantishna?"

"Came from McGrath, really, but I've been quite a while. You headed for Kantishna?"

"I'm going to the Iditarod. How's the dog feed? Can I get some at the Turk's?"

Nothing weighty, those conversations. We were complete strangers, but in a sparsely settled land each person has more value. You're glad to see each other. When you release your brake and your dogs perk up and yank the sled loose, you wave a mittened hand to your departing acquaintance with the warm feeling of a few shared moments. Even the dogs have taken on new life after a brief sniff of canine fellow travelers.

And you remember such meetings. Perhaps when the grass is green and the Arctic flora in full bloom, you see a fellow somewhere on the Yukon. "Say, I met you on the Koyukuk, remember? How'd you make out on that trip?"

Is it a hard life? Yes. In a roadhouse of an evening, when the stars are out in myriads and the logs are cracking with the cold, old-timers may cuss this "so-and-so" country. They are tired of falling into overflows up to their necks at forty below. "Why in hell didn't I stay in California? I didn't have to do this!"

Another may chime in: "Yeah, I lost a dog up there on the pass today. Froze to death right there in harness. Should know better than to use a bird dog on a trip like this."

But they didn't leave. The next fall their hands were again itching for the handlebars. They wanted once again to hear the hullabaloo when the dogs were being hooked up in the morning. Perhaps the Arctic winter had gotten into their blood. Low on the southern horizon in a sky of old rose, the sun tints the snow a faint pink. There's not much warmth in the winter sun, and it shines for just a few hours, but it's part of the wonder of the Arctic.

I was starting on a long trip and spent the first night at the roadhouse near the recently completed government railroad, on which the dogs and I had come to the south side of Broad Pass in the Alaska Range. I learned that the mailman was due any time, with his seventeen-dog team, and the old-timers were all waiting for him to go first to break the trail. I was new to Alaska and thought it was unfair to wait for someone else to go first and break trail. I decided to start out alone in the morning.

When I went out to hook up my team, I found that I had only four dogs left! One had been killed in a dog fight during the night. There I was, a stranger just learning the Alaska type of dog mushing, starting out for Rainy Pass in the Alaska Range and points far beyond—with only four dogs.

On this February morning in 1922 my objective was to reach the Rainy Pass country, a wintering ground of the caribou.

I met several travelers along the way, among them a United States marshal and a prisoner he was taking from McGrath out to the railroad (dogteam was the only means of travel). We stopped to pass the time of day, and I learned what the situation was. The prisoner didn't say much, but there was no sign of handcuffs or other legal paraphernalia. Up here, there seemed to be little distinction made between the lawman and the prisoner— they were just fellow travelers.

I had been warned to pass up the Mountain Climber Roadhouse if I possibly could, because even by frontier standards its accommodations were very poor. Besides, I was allowed only $5.50 per day for expenses, and road-houses charged two dollars per meal and two dollars for a bed. So I camped out whenever I could.

Accordingly, instead of going on to this roadhouse, I made an early camp. I tramped down the snow, put up my seven-by-nine tent, and set up my small Yukon stove. I chained the dogs to trees, out of reach of each other. They jumped and howled in anticipation as the salmon were being pulled out of the sled load. I tossed a dried salmon to each and with what wholesome gusto they tore at that fish, eating every morsel. Then, realizing there was no more coming, each curled up in his snowy nest, nose in tail, and slept.

I cooked my simple meal of bacon, rice, dried fruit, and "Jersey Creams," a tasty, softer "hardtack" widely used in Alaska. I didn't care for tea or coffee myself, but coffee was the universal drink in Alaska, as tea had been in Hudson Bay. After dinner I spread out my warm sleeping bag of woven rabbit skins from Hudson Bay, laid a little kindling for morning, blew out the candle, and soon I was snug for the night, like the dogs curled up out there in the snow.

In the morning it was storming, and I knew we faced heavy going, but fortunately I had learned about gee poles. I cut and trimmed off a small spruce tree, fastening it with rope and thongs under the right front end of the sled so that it slanted out at my hand height. Thus I could straddle the towline behind the dogs, become one of them, and guide the sled. Then the mailman, with his big seventeen-dog team, caught up with me, and he took the lead. From that point on, my four dogs trotted along gleefully, and we all made good time. In mid-afternoon we came to Mountain Climber, my companion's regular stop. We were met by the owner and put our dogs in the low kennels he had—I had lost all ambition to go on alone.

"I'm going after some wood. Go in and make yourself at home," the proprietor told us, and with an axe over his shoulder he strode off down a slope into the snowy woods.

We went inside and I looked around curiously. I was thirsty so I walked over to a pail with a dipper beside it. There was a little water in the pail, but it looked quite dingy. How many days ago had he fetched it? There were successive rims of ice in the pail down to the water, showing the level at which ice had frozen each night. But I was thirsty and used to such things, so I took a drink.

Then I happened to look out the window and saw the owner returning. The axe head was stuck in a chunk of wood, and he was carrying it with the axe handle over his shoulder. It seemed to me a very strange way of gathering wood.

We finally sat down to supper, and I wondered how it would be. But the mailman had been here often and was very pleasant and understanding. By suggestions and humorous remarks, he had our host bringing us a variety of food, including some cookies. So the next morning when we pushed on, I was not sorry we had stopped at Mountain Climber Roadhouse.

As we went along together on the trail that day, I was surprised to see a heavy gasoline engine on the mailman's sled. The charge for such freight was a dollar a pound. I wondered who wanted an engine that badly.

That same day I had another experience with his load. I was collecting specimens for the Biological Survey collection in Washington whenever I had opportunity. We saw a flock of ptarmigan on the snow in among the trees, and we stopped the two sleds. To get one of the birds, I pulled the shotgun out of the top of my load. The skin would be a specimen, and the meat would be my dinner.

Now whenever there was any sudden commotion, the dogs would get excited and go off on the run. No matter from what direction the diversion might come, they would keep to the trail and speed straight ahead. (They reacted the same way to the smell of game. When there was caribou scent in the air, we would make wonderful time as long as the scent lasted.) At the sound of my gun, my dogs started forward pell-mell, right up alongside the mail sled, and my gee pole pierced one of the mail sacks, bringing my sled to a sudden stop. Think of my dismay! The mailman was a friendly and understanding soul, noted my discomfiture, and did his best to put me at ease. But I have often wondered in what condition some of those letters reached their destination.

In a few days the mailman went on, and I stopped along the way to investigate the winter wildlife. In addition to studying the caribou, I was to report on the birds and mammals living in the areas I traveled. I was also commissioned as federal fur warden, and my district was interior and northern Alaska. I had little time or taste for the latter duty, but appropriations were small and we were short of personnel.

As I traveled over the lowland and up the outer slopes of the mountains, I enjoyed recording what I saw. I was pleased to see the chickadee among the lower branches of a spruce, always busy and much alive, adding a cheery note to any winter woods. This bird often came to the spruces near the trail, as if he too were glad to see someone. There was also the magpie, always aloof and wary, traits to be expected in a bird so persecuted by man. His dark body with striking stripes and patches of white gave a vivacious accent to the winter landscape. Then there were the tracks in the snow—tracks of squirrels, tiny shrews, and snowshoe hares. I knew there were wolverines, for now and then I saw the tracks of this elusive animal, too. At night I sometimes heard the great horned owl. All of this made me aware that underneath the apparent lifelessness in this wintry northland the landscape was still alive.

But I kept looking up to the higher mountains, the Rainy Pass country I was heading for. What would I find up there? When I arrived at the point where I was to leave the dog trail and go off into the desolate high caribou and mountain sheep country, I spent the night at an old-timer's cabin. For two days and nights I had suffered with a toothache, and I spoke of my trouble to my host, a pioneer Alaskan. Of course he had a remedy—a drastic one—if I wanted to take a chance on it.

"I'll tell you what I done once, and it helped. I put iodine on it. I got a bottle of iodine here."

I was horrified at the idea of putting pure iodine in my mouth, but I was desperate.

My friend brought out his little bottle of iodine and a ptarmigan feather to dip with. I took the feather and thoroughly smeared the gums on both sides of the aching tooth with iodine. Immediately the pain of the remedy was much greater than the toothache it was to cure, and I resolved not to swallow any of this poison, but that night I slept. Next morning all pain was gone. I had no more trouble until I reached Fairbanks and a dentist in the spring.

I always felt that the best part of my journeys came after I left the well-traveled dog trails. I had crossed the lowlands south of the mountains and gone through the Rainy Pass. Now there rose before me the high mountain country just north of the summit of the Alaska Range. From my maps and the verbal directions of roadhouse keepers, I knew about where I wanted to go. So off we went, the four dogs and I, to explore high mountains new to us.

As the days went by, I wondered what the dogs got out of it. I had a supply of dried salmon on the sled, and they eagerly looked forward to their meal each evening. They loved to be in harness; as a matter of fact, as they were being hooked up in the morning, they were so happy that it was hard to handle them. The minute we were ready, off they would go in a great burst of speed.

We encountered many obstacles as we went along, but the dogs seemed to take everything as a matter of course. When we came to the Rhone River, our route lay straight across it. It had been blown free of snow and there was glare ice. We were at the mercy of the elements. The dogs' feet had no traction, the sled swerved, and a few times we went round in a circle. Fortunately, the wind was at our backs, and somehow we drifted and slid across the ice river and continued on our journey.

As I lived with those four dogs and we shared the little vicissitudes of the trail, I was impressed with the thought that we human creatures share with dogs certain characteristics of behavior. There is a primeval truculence which appears at times—a real joy in the fight. I have seen my lead dog, Snook, sail into a mass of fighting dogs with what appeared to be a smile on his face. There was also the joy in simply being active that was so obvious on this trip. The dogs were eager to be up and doing, to go somewhere, to pull the sled. I had a similar feeling, wanting to clamber over the mountains, to discover, to achieve. I suppose we can say that both man and dog have the joyous impulse to *do*.

One day, from an old, deserted cabin where I had camped, I went up on a high mountain to look around. There I came upon a band of mountain sheep. Mindful of the needs of the museum on the other side of the continent, I obtained two of them for specimens. It was late in the day, and I was unable to finish and carry both back to camp. One sheep would have to be left overnight. But I had seen wolverine tracks and knew what to expect—the wolverine has been cursed as a trap robber, and our literature is full of lurid tales about the sins of this animal. Much of this has arisen because of our tendency to hate any animal that interferes with *us* in any way. I decided to make a bargain with the wolverine. I wanted the skin and skull for a specimen; the wolverine would want some meat to eat. So I partially skinned the animal, pulled the skin over the head, laying bare much of the carcass of pure meat. Then I filled my packsack with the other specimen and went down to camp.

Next morning I went back up the mountain for my specimen sheep. As I approached, two magpies flew off; those canny birds had found this source of food. Coming closer, I saw that the wolverine had been there, had his feed of meat, and gone his way. He had accepted the bargain; he had his meal, the museum would have its specimen, and the dogs and I still had a supply of camp food.

These were unforgettable days high above timberline, on slopes where I found the caribou spending the winter. This was one of the many places where these hardy Arctic travelers found they could paw down through the snow and find the tasty "reindeer moss," or lichens, below. Both forms of life, these particular lichens and the caribou, have found the Arctic a suitable place in which to live. This little alpine wintering place, high in the mountains of Rainy Pass, is one spot in the vast circumpolar Arctic that has nourished the caribou for many centuries.

I spent some time in this area, collected a caribou specimen, and weighed the animal with a steelyard that I carried in my pack. In nearby rugged uplands were bands of mountain sheep living serenely through the winter as they had done for many centuries.

It was hard for me to pull away from this peaceful Arctic-alpine paradise. But I had a mission to perform—to learn about the distribution of caribou in Alaska and Yukon—and I could not linger. So the four dogs and I started off for other parts. We went to visit domestic reindeer herds to the west, and eventually, about the middle of March, we were back on the mail trail, headed for Lake Minchumina and the Kantishna country.

At the last roadhouse I had hoped to get dog feed for the long trailless trip to the Kantishna, but the proprietor explained that he was obligated to serve only those who stopped at his place for the period of their stay, and could not undertake to outfit a longer expedition. But he did tell me all he could about the route. Someone had been through and had headed in that direction about a week before. "He musta left a sled track. I hope you can find that sled track most of the time. It will help you."

So I started off next morning, short of dog feed and with only a vague notion of where I was going. But over on my right, far away, rose lofty Mount McKinley, called by the Indians *Denali* ("The Highest One"), and Mount Foraker beside it. These would guide me. By going eastward, I hoped to reach the Kantishna River by the end of March.

I had good fortune. I came upon an occasional Indian camp and moved along steadily. Yet the going was difficult, and the dogs had lost all their enthusiasm. Theirs was hard, steady, never-ending work. Finally Jack, my old standby in the team, became so tired that I had to take him out of his harness and let him run loose. Then I had only three dogs and myself to wrestle with the sled. Most Alaskan travelers had five to seven dogs, at the least. Moreover, I was reduced to sharing my own food supply with the dogs, and we were all living on very meager rations. I could find no rabbits but I shot an occasional ptarmigan (using the big rifle since I was short of shotgun shells) so that the dogs could have at least a little meat.

One day I met an Indian coming along the faint trail, and we had a good visit. Most important, he gave me a moose heart, and I lived on this for several days. He also gave me good directions, mentioning a lake as a landmark. As I started off, he warned me, "Watch out dat lake. Big fish stop dere!" I thanked him for his warning, but as I went on, I wondered about the belief in a mythical spirit fish that lived in a frozen lake. It seems inherent in the human mind to reach into the spirit world and create myths.

Those days sound tough and desperate in the telling, and I wonder whether it is misleading to relate such experiences on paper. Yes, we were all hungry, but the dogs took it philosophically (they can work for a couple of days without any food, I have found), and somehow I don't remember that I felt badly either. Kantishna and supplies lay ahead somewhere. And I remember the inspiration I got from seeing those great mountains off on the horizon.

Occasionally in the evening we would see the aurora. The dogs took no notice, but for me the lights never lost their excitement.

Part of this time we had wind and cloudiness, but I recall one night when it was still and clear, and close to forty degrees below zero. I knew it would not storm on such a night. I fed the dogs some ptarmigan meat and ate a little of the moose heart myself. I didn't bother to put up the tent but simply spread out my sleeping bag, took off my boots, and crawled in, parka and all. For some reason this clear, cold night remains vividly in my memory. As I lay there, cozy and warm in the sleeping bag, the four dogs curled up close around the edges of my bed, life seemed good. We had a special comradeship, camping and traveling together.

One day we came to an Indian camp. The trail they had made lay among their tents—and their dogs. Ordinarily, strange dogs will fight, but my four were hungry. They paid no attention to the bedlam of those chained dogs, but pushed eagerly forward, their noses alive for any scent of food. I got the team through to the edge of the village, and after a brief visit with the Indians, we went on.

I was entering a more inhabited region now. Soon I came to another well-worn trail, at right angles to my course. Which way? I decided to go to the right, but just then heard dogs howling off to the left. My dogs pulled in that direction, so I changed my mind and turned left. Soon we came to another Indian village, where we learned that we were now headed for Tanana. With new information about the trail, we turned around and took the direction of my first, instinctive choice. We could not make it to any settlement that night and again camped out. There was just a little bite to eat all around—the last of the moose heart.

On March 22 we reached a little place called Roosevelt on the map, with a few old miners' cabins. I noted in my official diary: "Clear again today. I went on and early in the morning reached Roosevelt, where I was invited to stop by Mr. Einar Hansen."

Here was plenty to eat. The dogs tore at the whole quarter of meat Mr. Hansen provided. To replenish his supplies, he and I took our rifles down to a frozen stream and shot moose. He was in meat again, and we were all well fed.

Now I was back on a traveled dog trail, back in easy living. With comfortable travel, I reached the railroad at Nenana on March 30, after crossing the flats for forty miles.

On that last night in the Kantishna country there was another great display of the aurora—a colorful farewell to a long trip in the wilderness surrounding Denali.

Pooto and His Family

In 1922 my brother Adolph had come north to be my assistant in the caribou study, and we were scheduled to travel to several places on the Yukon River, then up into the Koyukuk River country and into the Brooks Range, and back by way of the Chandalar River valley and the Yukon again. It would be a long trip, a great circuit which would measure at least fifteen hundred miles, and we were anxious to get started. But the snow came late that fall around Fairbanks, and we had to have snow. It was not until November 24 that we boarded the train at Fairbanks, with dogs and sleds in the baggage car, and rode to Nenana. There we unloaded and set off over a rough trail to Tanana on the Yukon, still with barely enough snow for sledding.

This part of our trip was taken up with routine matters, such as purchasing supplies and more dogs to add to our two teams. From Tanana we went down the Yukon toward Kokrines, where we were to make a routine survey of a domestic reindeer herd some miles inland from that point.

Our first day on the Yukon stands out in my memory. We were traveling in the short, dark winter days, and there was bright moonlight when we had finished breakfast at "Daddy" Black's roadhouse at Tanana and had gone out to harness the dogs. They were lively and unruly after three days of rest, and Daddy Black stood on the brake of one sled while we got the wriggling, jumping animals into harness. I had a good leader and went first.

Adolph followed behind. Daddy Black led my team to the bank of the Yukon, then let them go. He shouted good-bye as we hurtled down the steep bank. My leader swung onto the trail, and we were off.

But suddenly my team of seven was a writhing, snarling mass of fighting dogs. They loved to fight! I seized a chain and luckily managed to beat them apart before real damage was done. The dogs quieted down, and I had time to consider our surroundings. The broad Yukon stretched away in the bright, mellow moonlight, and the other shore was a low, dark line in the distance. We threaded the edge of the rough ice near one bank. The dogs trotted steadily along, an indistinct blur of moving furry figures—the whole thing a page from a fantasy. And here I was—mushing a team of malamutes! How I gloried in the feeling! Ade said nothing, but I am sure he was feeling the same emotions.

Dawn approached. The moon sank lower and lower to a high bluff fringed with bare cottonwoods, and as the daylight slowly wiped away the magic, the moon sank out of sight in a silvery haze. Behind us, her rival the sun began to show his colors, a dim gold on the horizon, which grew and spread in rich and richer hues. But it seemed loath to appear and we traveled far with lingering glances to the glory of the horizon until mid-forenoon, when the sun burst into view and gilded the ice, the trees, and the distant hills. But it lingered along the horizon and in a very few hours dipped again out of sight. The short, northern day would soon be gone.

One night we stopped at a roadhouse run by a squaw man. His Indian wife silently prepared dinner, waited on us, and as silently cleared away the dishes—she was only a squaw, who had no business talking to strange white men. But later, as we sat around the stove, we engaged her in conversation, and she told us about her nine-year-old daughter Irene, who was attending school at Tanana. She brought out a photograph of the little girl and showed me a letter the child had written. Irene had been a big help about the house and in her letter asked her mother how she got the dishes washed now. This little girl also wrote letters to her dog, and the mother told us that one time Paddy Carroll, the mail carrier, placed the pencil in the dog's paw and had him write a letter to the little girl. Irene wanted her mother to come up for the coming Christmas program, as she had several parts in the program and wanted help with her costumes. Her mother told us that she quite often took her dogteam and drove up to Tanana for a weekend, a distance of thirty-four miles.

There seemed to be a feeling that an Indian squaw, to use the common term of the country, was not a desirable companion for life. I often wondered about the taste of the squaw man and what manner of life he led. From what I saw, he was a simple fellow, satisfied with material things. He made a meager living by fishing, trapping, or driving a mail team, a hand-to-mouth existence, yet he seemed comfortable. And from what I saw, his home life appeared pleasant enough. He loved his children, and the family was generally happy and contented, with the same amount of scandal as that in a white community. We are all people, with the same human impulses. Later on I became acquainted with another mixed family, in which the mutual feelings were of the best.

The sentiment shown in the case of little Irene gave me a pleasant feeling about such a home. I never heard a squaw man express himself on the subject, but there seemed to exist a certain amount of sentiment and love and a kind of rough tenderness in this household. And little Irene was getting an education, which we all need.

On our side trip to Kokrines and beyond, one incident stands out. We were going peacefully along the trail with our teams when, from the other direction, there came a different kind of sleigh, a wide one, with a man driving a reindeer hitched to it. Our dogs immediately wanted to give battle—here was an ancestral prey animal! We had to shove our teams quickly into the willows beside the trail, entangling the harnesses and towlines in the brush, so we could let the reindeer go by. The dogs had not before seen such a sight, and that was the only reindeer pulling a sled that I ever saw in Alaska.

It was December 20 before we came back up the Yukon to Tanana and started into the Koyukuk country. We did not follow the rivers and in a short time were on the overland trail north to Allakaket.

On this part of our journey we had more dog fights, one of which ended in a tragedy. One of the husky dogs that I had purchased on the Tanana was so severely bitten that it would have taken him most of the winter to recover. A front foot pad was split in two. We finally decided that the humane thing to do was to put Brownie out of his misery. I took off his harness, took the rifle off the sled, led him off into a grove of trees, and left him there. Ade said that at the sound of the shot, the other dogs pricked up their ears, but I am sure they did not understand.

On the first part of the Koyukuk trail we had a strenuous time. It was uphill, the sleds overturned many times, the dogs were ill-tempered, and I nearly despaired of further progress. Freezing perspiration whitened my parka hood, and I finally discarded it.

However, when we reached the top of the first hills and looked out across new valleys before us, I forgot the petty vexations and thrilled with the somber beauty of it. One could see distant ridges, wide slopes, and little ravines tracing down into the greater streams, all snowy, with long, thin lines of trees seeking cover in the nooks and sheltered places. And far off, mingling with the cold blue clouds, were the misty, deeper blue mountains.

As we went over the top of a high hill, a cold, penetrating breeze met us—indeed, near the close of the short Arctic day, the whole aspect, cold blue and gray and white with an accent of black in the strips of forest, was chilling. But we were looking up toward the Arctic, with the Arctic Circle, only a few days ahead, and the incentive to explore new valleys and have new experiences neutralized the cold and made of it but a spice in the adventure.

The snow here was drifted, and we slipped and bumped along over the drifts on the long downward slope into the heart of the new landscape. There in the woods we came upon a little cabin we had heard about, where we gratefully spent the night, snug and comfortable. From my journal:

> Dec. 21: "The shortest day, and a very pleasant one. In these short days we cannot help noticing the sky. This day the sky was cloudy dull slate, brightened by occasional streaks of lighter hue— pale gleams of blue and lavender or dull yellow.

"We crossed an interesting barrens—wide, almost level stretches of tundra and gently sloping plains. These opens somehow impressed me profoundly; I wanted to linger and assimilate the full beauty of them. I do not know in what it consists, the charm of it all. Perhaps the dogteams trotting along, threading a ribbon trail across it, belonged in the picture. I thought of herds of caribou dotting such a scene. Certainly the wildness of it and the expanse of it seemed to require some wide-ranging animals and perhaps therein lay its charm for me. I seemed to want to roam over these plains myself, like the caribou, and feed on lichens, face the winds, and travel on and on."

From my journal of December 22 I shall quote only one short sentence: "What wonderful clouds in Alaska!"

December 24—another Christmas in the Far North. We spent that evening in a small trail cabin. There was no Santa Claus or any of the customary holiday trimmings, but nature helped to make this a special and

beautiful day. The sunrise itself was striking. A heavy cloud reached up from the horizon, widening and spreading the higher it reached, in the shape of a tornado. It was all aflame, a deep fire red at the horizon, throwing a ruddy flush here and there over the great cloud mass, and tinting the little flecks of cloud scattered beyond. It was like a flaming banner, which could well make us think of the aftermath of that first Christmas. A star showed furtively on one side.

The evening, too, helped to celebrate Christmas on this short winter day. A bright crescent moon cast a tracery of shadows in the forest, silvering the snow and trees. And the stars blinked brightly, adding to the crispness of the evening. An enchanting scene.

We had gone only seventeen miles that day. In the little cabin in the wilderness, we cooked up some of the best food we had and opened the gifts we had received from friends in Fairbanks. We took our dogs into the cabin, two or three at a time, for a special treat, to enjoy scraps of dainties. Our thoughts went especially to the dear ones we had left far south. To add a little to our celebration, we had taken in a small top of a spruce and hung tallow candles on it, one for each of our family members back in Minnesota and our Fairbanks friends. It seemed a real Christmas when we lit them all.

Next day we knew we would get to Allakaket, the Episcopal mission of St. John's in the Wilderness. Adolph went ahead with his team that Christmas Day, and I came along some distance behind, as the two teams did not work well when too close together.

We reached Allakaket by early moonlight, about four o'clock, and stopped in the Kobuk Eskimo village. This was on the west side of the Koyukuk River, where Sam Dubin's trading post was. Across the Koyukuk, still pretty wide at this point, was the mission and the Indian village. We were told that our quarters would be upstairs over the store. The storekeeper and the trader were over at the mission, but the Eskimos who met us assured us that we were perfectly welcome and gave us a generous helping of caribou meat for our supper. How welcome they made us feel!

They were all leaving for the Christmas tree party at the mission, so we also shaved and cleaned up as best we could in our travel togs. On our way into the hall, two young native boys gave us each a bag of candy and told us where to find the Christmas tree. We arrived too late to see Santa Claus—he had just finished his duties—but the tree was there, and the hall was full of Eskimos and Indians, along with two women missionaries, the trader, and his storekeeper. They all flocked around to shake our hands and greet us with "Merry Christmas!"

At one of the mail cabins where we had stopped along the trail, we had found a set of false teeth some traveler had left behind. We had taken them along in a baking powder can and had given them to one of the Eskimos going ahead of us to the program. Some of them knew that the teeth belonged to Sam Dubin, the trader, who had come over the trail just ahead of us, and they were presented to him by Santa Claus!

A few evenings later the Eskimos and Indians again gathered in the dance hall near the mission. I appreciated the fact that a dance hall was provided for these people through the cooperation of the mission, an unusual and helpful thing. Ade and I went over with some of the friendly Eskimos to watch.

A group of men were assembled near a drum they had purchased, to take the place of their own native drums. They sang a song, every line or two repeating a "a-hung-a-ya-ya, hung-a-ha-ya-ya." (At least it sounded something like that, and seemed to correspond to our "tra-la-la.") Then a tall young Kobuk stepped out in front. He wore on his head a circle of the neck of a loon, the head and the bill sticking out over his forehead. He wore gloves with little straps fastened on the backs, to fool the evil spirit if he should try to seize him. He danced in the one-two rhythm, hopping about in various attitudes, his hands pointing here and there, also in rhythm. Occasionally, he uttered a vigorous "Uh-hu-hu!" in a loud voice. After a while some Eskimo women came out at one side and accompanied him by swaying with the rhythm.

When the Eskimos were through with several dances, the Indians did their dance. It seemed a somber affair, an even, marching shuffle with a simple rhythm. The Indian who led the dance had lost a son the summer before, and I suppose the almost monotone singing recounted that affair.

When they were through with their dance, that same Indian and his wife sat down in an adjacent room where they had a pile of their belongings. According to their custom, they were to give away all they owned and start life again with nothing. They had a couple of children who took each article and went with it to the designated person, until all was given away. When we went out, I noticed that at least two or three of the Eskimos dropped a half-dollar down in the lap of the Indian woman.

On another evening Adolph and I went over when they were doing white man's dances. We just sat there and watched, since we were not dancers and did not want to take part. A tall, handsome young native was calling the dances. He had a sense of humor, for he would call out, "Get your partners for a fox trap!"

Again he would call, "Get your partners for fadrille!"

Several came over and urged that we go out and take part in a square dance; but we were afraid we would only disrupt things, since we knew nothing about square dancing. Presently the announcer called out, "Get your partners for fadrille. Ladies' choice!" Two young Eskimo girls came straight across the floor to us and asked: "Will you dance with us?"

We could hardly refuse, so we went with them and joined a square dance. It certainly seemed confusing, but somehow they pushed us around where we were supposed to go, and we did finish the dance. We were elated by our success, and I am sure it pleased those who had cooked up the plot.

One evening we went over to a meeting of the Eskimos. At one point old Tobuk, the chief, was speaking in Eskimo, and I could not understand all the Kobuk dialect. I was sitting far in the back of the group and was surreptitiously making sketches in my notebook of some of the people.

After a while a young Eskimo came back to speak to me. "They have caught me at it," I thought, "and now want to object to what I am doing." But the young Eskimo wanted to translate for us what old Tobuk had just said: "We appreciate you white men coming over and taking part with us. It makes us happy and you are most welcome!"

We stayed at Allakaket a number of days, asking the people about caribou and other aspects of natural history. Here we became acquainted with

Pooto, a Kobuk who had come down from his cabin up the Alatna River. One day Pooto said something that at first I could not understand: he told me he didn't care for the Alatna River. "It's awful country," he said. "Too much timber. I can't see far. I think go back Arctic side. Noatak my country. There see far."

We are not all alike. What we appreciate depends on where and how we grew up. Coming up here from the Yukon River, we had taken pleasure in the beauty that surrounded us, in the forests as well as the open plains.

WE WERE DESTINED TO KNOW POOTO AND HIS FAMILY BETTER THAN WE had anticipated. At Allakaket we had made plans to go up to his cabin and later farther north. On January 4 we said good-bye to Hank the storekeeper and other new friends in the village, and traveled on up the Alatna River to Pooto's home, two days' journey away. There we met Pooto's wife, Annie, who could not speak English, and his three children, the oldest a boy of twelve.

When we arrived at Pooto's, we were just ahead of a severe cold spell. We could hear our breath hissing as it passed our ears, so we knew it was at least fifty degrees below zero. Later we learned that at Allakaket they had recorded sixty-eight degrees below. During this time the dogs crouched all curled up deep in the snow. In Pooto's one-room cabin Ade and I were given a place in one corner to spread our sleeping bags, on the floor. In this intimate association, we learned more about Eskimos.

Pooto showed me a slender ivory handle of an Eskimo drill, decorated in a long line by figures of various birds carved into the handle. I recognized a crane and a loon. He also showed me a similar handle of a "tool bag" with figures carved in a line, each of them showing the flukes of a beluga whale that the hunter had killed. These two articles had been made by Pooto's great-grandfather, over on the Noatak River. Pooto said that in those days the Eskimos shot birds with bow and arrow, sometimes in flight.

Mary, Pooto's young daughter, was using a spoon made from a mountain sheep horn. Later, when we left the country, she gave me her spoon as a gift.

During these cold days of staying close to home, we learned of some Eskimo superstitions and stories. Pooto told me that one time a bear started down toward the earth from way up in the sky. As he came falling down, he became smaller and smaller until, when he landed in the snow, he became the lemming. He declared that the lemming track has the same pattern as that of a bear, which substantiated the story. And another Eskimo passing through told me that he had seen the hole in the snow where the falling lemming had come down. I didn't argue; I just wrote down what they told me.

There came a break in the weather, and Ade and I planned to make our trip over to the Kobuk River. Pooto went with us to a high ridge and pointed out to us certain mountains in the distance that would lead us to the upper reaches of the Kobuk. We started off and luckily took a compass bearing on those mountains. In the following days as we traveled into strange country, the air was full of falling snow, and we did not see the mountains again.

I was realizing what a good outdoorsman my young brother was, and on this trip to the Kobuk I was amazed at how easily he took to snowshoes. We had to do a lot of trail-breaking ahead of the dogs as we made our way through this trackless region, and Ade took to it like an old sourdough. I recalled how I had stumbled around the first time I had put on snowshoes, years before in the Oregon Cascades.

After a few days we reached the head of the Kobuk and looked over the country ahead. All the way over we had seen no caribou or other animals. We decided not to go down the Kobuk—there were so many other places on our itinerary. We turned back and followed our good sled track back to the cabin and the Pooto family.

After our return there was another cold spell, and as we all waited at the cabin, we were again privileged to see the home life of these modern Eskimos. The mere fact that Pooto had a log cabin revealed the white man's influence, but these people still kept some of their old customs. For one thing, they ate raw, frozen fish. That white fish meat looked so appetizing that one day I tried some. When it had thawed in my mouth, however, I discovered that it had not been frozen soon enough. I did not try it again. One day Annie boiled some bear feet, wristlets of fur still on them—we didn't mind appearances, and they tasted good.

One evening Pooto was speaking in his language to the children. The way he was talking, I thought he was telling a story. When he finished I asked, "Pooto, was that a story you were telling?"

He mumbled yes but seemed surprised.

"Will you tell me the story so I can take it down, and the little song too?"

Pooto hesitated, and I surmised that he would assume that the white man would think his story not worth telling. So I said, "We have stories, too, that we tell to our children."

And I told him the old fairy tale of the fox that induced a bear to put his tail down through a hole in the ice to catch fish. When the tail froze solid in the ice, the fox told him to pull hard and he would get some fish. The bear pulled hard, and pulled off his tail. Ever since then the bear has had only a short stump of a tail. Pooto laughed, and immediately told the story to Annie in Eskimo, and she laughed heartily. After that I had no trouble getting Pooto's story of how a ground squirrel outwitted a raven, and I got the little song in Eskimo, too. Then he told us another story, of how a snowy owl drowned trying to cross a stream carrying a rock; there was a song with this one, too. I told Pooto I wanted to write them down so I would not forget. He was interested and asked me to repeat the stories and corrected me on some points; he was now enthusiastic and elaborated on some parts. When I learned the song in Eskimo, they all laughed and seemed delighted to hear a white man singing in their language.

A few days later, we were all out on a short trip with the dogteams and had stopped to rest. Suddenly Pooto laughed heartily and said, "Pretty foxy fox, awright! He freeze 'em off te de tail de bear!"

At the cabin we became familiar with the children, so familiar that Mary began joking with us. Several times in the morning she got up before we did and would call across to us, "*Sinook-puk-tutin* ('You're sleeping too much')." We became as one family, occupying that little cabin. And then there was an incident which showed how much we trusted one another.

Pooto and I had gone upriver with a load of dogfish, using his team. An old dog in the wheel, a female, was lagging. Pooto explained that she was about fifteen years old and had been a wonderful dog in her day, but was no longer useful. The people in the Far North can't afford to keep and feed a dog that is not working. He hinted that he would like to have her killed. Presently I realized what was on his mind. She was not attached to me, and much as I disliked shooting any dog, I realized how he felt and offered to do it for him. "I will do a good job of it," I assured him.

He eagerly accepted my offer. "I kill my dog before, awright," he explained, "but dis one I no like kill 'em. I keep 'em long time—I guess fifteen years. He good dog one time," and he went on dwelling on the virtues of the dog in her younger days.

Next morning I said to Pooto, "I'll take your dog now."

"Wait," he said, and went in to Annie. The two of them came from the cache with half a frozen rabbit and gave it to the dog.

"I like give 'em last feed before kill 'em," he said.

The dog soon finished the meal, and Annie went back into the cabin. Pooto then told me I could take the dog, admonishing me, "Go way down river, so Annie she don't hear." I did as he requested and he was spared the pain of killing his favorite dog.

We wanted to get some mountain sheep specimens from the Brooks Range for the National Museum and asked Pooto if he would be our guide. He thought it over, then made us another proposition. We would all go up there, he suggested. He would take his family along; he would get all the meat, and we could have the skins and skulls. We agreed to that arrangement. He said he could not start for a couple of days, but we could start out and he would send his son Angiok to guide us. He and the rest of the family would soon catch up with us.

On February 15 we started out. The sun came out bright and clear, a delightful day among mountains, creeks, and lakes. At one point, while we were resting on Helpmejack Creek, a little weasel came up to investigate our sleds, and Jake, in Ade's team, pricked up his ears with keen interest. Later seeing an otter gave me a thrill. What other animals were hidden away here?

I thought of the wolverine, fox, and lynx, all living somewhere in these woods.

When we had traveled on for a while, our guide, twelve-year-old Angiok, became confused. He hunted around a bit, then confessed, "I lose 'em trail."

I did not want to say anything to interfere with his mental processes, so stood quietly. Soon he said to me, "Oh *my*, I lose 'em trail!" He wanted me to understand clearly that he was lost.

"Angiok, where do you *think* we ought to go?" I suggested. "Let's go where we think it's best to go."

We were supposed to come to a lake. I pointed ahead in a certain direction. "The lake that way, you think?"

"Yeh," he replied.

"We make trail that way, then," I said. "You think that's all right?"

"I guess," he replied, and I decided to go ahead anyway, as there seemed to be but one general route that was reasonable to me. Little Angiok brightened when he saw me take the initiative but made one suggestion: "Maybe lots of willows." I hoped that would not be the case, as that always meant hard going.

I steered straight ahead through the spruce forest, picking my way through the open lanes and praying that the trail would continue open and clear. Occasionally Angiok seemed to remember a little and suggested going one way or another. And after about an hour he joyfully pointed to an old blaze on a tree. "My mamma's papa make dat mark long time 'go."

Now he became quite talkative, and I could appreciate his evident relief—our twelve-year-old guide was on the right trail.

That night it was cold, and we slept fitfully in our tent, squirming and twisting in our sleeping bags. As we hovered over the little Yukon stove in the morning to cook our breakfast, we made various remarks about Alaska. "Who wants to live in such a country? What's it good for anyway? It's always eternally cold! Wait till we get back south again! . . ."

Presently we packed up our gear, took down the tent, and loaded the sleds. With our shelter gone, I felt that we were out in a very cold world. As we took the dogs out from their beds, they uncoiled reluctantly and would have preferred to remain curled up to keep warm. We quickly got under way, and with the exercise of the trail, both men and dogs were soon warm. Then I noticed what a fine day it really was. The short days were past, and it was still, with clear, bright sunshine. It was now near the end of February, and as the sun rose higher, we began to feel its warmth. Presently we had a good view of mountains up ahead—the purest white with dark blue timber at their bases, the summits varied and marked with delicate snow shadows. Those great mountains stand there, solid, massive, silent, waiting eternally in the still, bright sunshine. Like majestic cathedrals, these snowy peaked mountains impressed me with the sacred quiet of a sabbath.

Later in the day I saw little wisps of drifting snow curling like smoke about the shoulders of some of the high peaks. The wind grew gradually stronger. Before long the snow was sweeping along in streamers, and clouds appeared and wrapped the mountains in a haze. After we made camp that night, the growing storm flapped and tore at our tent, and the trees about us swayed and moaned. I felt that the mountains had come to life—there was no longer that passive, resting quiet. How weather, and our feelings, can change in a single day!

Pooto, with the rest of the family, caught up with us. On his advice we went up the Kutuk River, within easy distance of some mountain sheep ranges. Here Ade and I hoped to get our sheep specimens and Pooto his meat.

This was a new world, and from Pooto we learned many things. We found that the high, snowy slopes were frozen hard, and Pooto advised us to use canes, or "alpenstocks," made of a pole cut in the woods near our base camp, sharpened at one end. These we found most useful in getting over the hard mountain slopes.

One day I had an amazing experience. We found that in going down those steep slopes, Pooto would lie down, put his stick down through the center opening in his snowshoes, put his weight above the stick which acted like a brake, and down the slope he would go with everything under control. We came to one such slope one day, and Pooto and Ade both went down easily. When my turn came, however, my weight somehow moved off center. I lost all control, and finally turned over on my back and slid down at a terrific speed. I don't know how far down that mountain I would have gone, but there was a big, soft snowdrift right near Pooto. I penetrated that drift full speed—swoosh! I was nearly buried in snow, but I was stopped. As I crawled out of the drift and began to shake off the snow, I heard Pooto laughing, "You savvy dat kind, awright!"

There came a day when we saw three rams up among the cliffs and carefully figured out our strategy. Ade and Pooto were to stalk the sheep directly. I was to take a roundabout route, up a long ridge and over to a long slope where I could meet the sheep if they fled from the other two hunters.

We started out. After quite a while I reached the highest point and wanted to hurry over to the slope where we had thought the fleeing sheep would go. However, as I started down the slope, I must have slipped. I went down all right—but left one snowshoe on top! So I had to laboriously climb up another slope to rescue my snowshoe. Just before I got over to the desired ridge, I heard some rifle fire. When I got there, I saw no sheep and wondered if they had gone by.

After a while, when I had gone way down the ridge, I saw Pooto. He called to me and asked if I had seen any sheep going up. They missed them, I thought feeling disappointed and chagrinned. But when I came up to Pooto, he announced with a chuckle, "We got all three of us, Olaus."

His ungrammatical sentence gave me great relief. They had got all three rams. We went to work getting the rams down off the cliffs, taking care of them, and snowshoed back to camp long after dark.

These were cold days. We had a pair of binoculars, which caught Pooto's fancy tremendously. Sometimes on a high ridge, he would sit there on the snow a long time, looking with the glasses over into mountains where he saw sheep, but too far away for us. He just wanted to look and to see. Ade and I would wait impatiently, huddled behind a ridge or drift, stomping around trying to keep from freezing. We were impatient with Pooto, but now I can appreciate his pleasure in seeing those mountains and the mountain sheep clearly for the first time.

We had an opportunity to experience the home life of these Eskimos, in camp and in their cabin. We hear a lot recently about teenage delinquency, about the attitude of parents toward their children. Among the Eskimos, in those early days, where they had not yet come in contact with the low stratum of white civilization, I saw no difficulty with the children. I suppose much of it was the result of the sparse and scattered population, where each one could have dignity and be an individual, not a mere cog in a human machine.

I was interested one evening by what Pooto said about his son Angiok. He asked me how he could help in Angiok's future. What could he do? I was puzzled by such a question. How could I know what to do? If Angiok should go far south to school, I wondered what companionship he would fall into. He was only twelve years old and already a good woodsman, and as far as I could see had all the human qualities I could admire. Finally I said, "Pooto, of course you want to give him all the education you can, down at Allakaket or somewhere else. But the main thing you can do, I think, is to encourage him in every way you can to grow up to be a good man, someone you can be proud of. I don't know the real answer; it's hard to say. But that is the way I feel." Many years later, when I was traveling on the Yukon, I heard good reports about Angiok.

Getting sheep specimens proved to be quite a chore. Going out there on the mountain ridges was a cold, rigorous job. Ade and I went out on alternate days, and Pooto went out every day. It turned out that Ade and Pooto got the other specimens.

Another problem was that we ran out of "white grub," as Pooto called it. In that cold weather we began to crave fat and cereal food of any kind. Before we ran out completely, Ade began making lard sandwiches with the Jersey Cream biscuits we still had. Finally, we had only mountain sheep meat. It was March and the sheep were lean. We had all the meat we could use, but no fat. All of us began to feel weak. We learned something about nutrition in the Arctic, and I realized why Eskimos are so fond of blubber.

On March 10 we broke camp and started southward. In our weakened condition we had a laborious time. The dogs, too, were tired. There had been snowstorms south of us, obliterating the trail we had made, and again we had to break trail ahead of the dogs. How well I remember that last day in to the cabin. For a while Angiok broke trail ahead of the teams, but we were going so slowly that we knew we had to do something else. So we put our two sleds and dogteams together, and Ade drove the combination. Pooto and his family came behind. I went ahead breaking trail, trying to find the old trail. I could not see any sign of the old trail, but I could feel it through the top snow. The snow on the sides was loose and soft, whereas the old trail was a harder core. And so we plodded on. It became dark, and I experimented by closing my eyes at times as I went along. It made no difference. About nine o'clock in the evening, after several hours of darkness, we finally saw the cabin ahead of us. Dogs and people alike were all tuckered out. How good the bed on the floor was that night!

Next day Pooto remembered that they had thrown some old potatoes out in the snow. He dug around and found them—anything for a different kind of food. After a fervent good-bye to Annie and the children, I left with my team the next morning. I gave Pooto one of my dogs as a present. A few days later Ade and Pooto arrived at Alatna.

Ade and I could not linger now; we had a long way yet to go. We settled our account with Pooto, bade him a warm good-bye, and on March 24 were on the trail again, this time north to Wiseman. From then on we had a good trail; we were on the mail route. We did not stop long at any place but talked with all the natives and pioneers we met about the whereabouts of caribou herds.

In a few days we were in Wiseman, the main settlement of the Koyukuk valley. Shortly thereafter we started for the Yukon River again along forks of the Chandalar River. At Fort Yukon on the Arctic Circle we were told that the spring breakup of ice on the Porcupine River, which flows into the Yukon there, is spectacular. One man told us he had once seen fourteen or fifteen caribou on a big cake of ice, floating downstream.

It was the middle of April, and we knew we would have to race to get back to Fairbanks on the snow. We went on up the Yukon to Circle, then overland to Circle Hot Springs, a roadhouse and primitive sort of spa run by an old-timer. Here we had a good bath, the first real one I could remember having that winter!

The snow was becoming soft and thawing in the daytime, which meant very hard going. So we traveled as much as possible at night and into the early morning, when the snow would freeze a bit. By now there was no darkness, but it did get cooler during the "night."

During that long winter trip, Ade had only three dogs in his team, but they were all very large and strong. Two of them, Jake and Jumbo, were quarter-breed wolves; the leader was a huge yellow dog called Irish, who weighed about 150 pounds. Those three took his sled and load easily.

One day on the trail, we were entertained by a snow bunting. Several of them were picking away on the ground. I whistled to a male near me. He hopped onto a clod nearby and began to sing. I whistled and he sang—it was a duet. We kept this up for a long time, until I had to quit and move on. Spring was coming, and it was time we got home with our sleds.

We had one more memorable experience before our trip ended. As we were going over Eagle Summit, we saw a big herd of caribou on a neighboring slope. We estimated that there were close to two thousand. All winter we had heard others speak of seeing caribou, but this was the first real herd we had actually seen.

We arrived in Fairbanks on April 26, traveling on the last snow. We had had an unforgettable five months.

Nest Life on the Tundra

In March 1924, I started out on another assignment. I took a large party from Fairbanks to the treeless shores of Bering Sea to study the habits of the abundant birdlife which nested there. The trip involved about 800 miles of dogteam travel and lasted from March until August. The last few days of it—across from the Yukon to the Bering Sea—remain in my mind as typical of hard going on the coastal tundra of Alaska.

We left the Yukon in the gathering storm with seven heavily loaded dogteams. As we hooked up the dogs, we could see Kusilvak Mountain, our one landmark, rising from the level tundra. As one team after another drew out on the Yukon, a haze crept up from the horizon, the wind swept down from the north, and the mountain disappeared. Soon we could not even see the riverbank. All the teams gathered on the south bank before starting across the trackless tundra, and a regular marching order was formed. We agreed to keep in sight of one another. One Eskimo guide led the way, and another Eskimo followed him. It was with mingled feelings of misgiving and adventure that I headed into the haze, the storm stinging my face around the edge of my parka hood. The teams ahead were a line of dim, dwindling blotches in the whirling snow. Occasionally a light, clear-cut disk glowed through the storm overhead, but then dark masses of haze blotted it out.

Our course would take us along a frozen slough, then over tundra into a lake, then another slough, grinding monotonously over the cold snow—hard going for the dogs, cold traveling for the men.

After endless winding through a long slough called Black River, we turned a point and found an Eskimo village—two cabins perched on the bank. This was far enough for one day. We tied our dogs in a patch of willows, and our party rented one cabin for the night while its owners moved into the other hut nearby.

The next day was in many ways a repetition of the first. A strong wind still swept over the flats, but the sunshine overhead cheered us. As we ground along, however, the storm increased, until a low drift was sweeping across the tundra, at times hiding the other dogteams from view. But overhead the sun was still bright, except occasionally when the snow fog would sweep over us. A steady, weary struggle—Kusilvak Mountain faded away. Then, as I climbed a bank, I saw an odd collection of stakes, tripods, and mounds. I realized we were coming to the Eskimo village of Monomik. Two huts, partly underground, were inhabited; several others were broken down and drifted over with snow. A few dogs cowered around us. The whole scene presented a cheerless, windswept prospect after a day's fight with the storm.

We tied some of the dogs up in the willows, some in the wretched huts. We took up our quarters in one of the huts—a greasy, filthy room reeking of seal oil and fish. But we managed to pass a comfortable night.

Still one more day of it—the everlasting driving snow and cold! We could not see the Askinuk Mountains on the coast, which should have been our landmark, but with the help of the Eskimos we got a compass bearing and struck blindly across. Toward evening the younger dogs began to play out, and even the older dogs lay down at every opportunity. My wise old leader curled up at every stop to conserve his energy for the long grind ahead. Finally, in the dusk of evening, the coastal mountains loomed up in the storm. At one point we could dimly see the masts of a tiny schooner, drifted over with snow, and then, around a point, we came upon the trading post which was our goal for that day.

Dick Negus, the trader, had been called to Nome for trial for the murder of an Eskimo. When we all filed into the house, his Eskimo wife cowered in fear in a corner. We assured her we meant no harm, told her that we had heard that her husband had been acquitted, and eventually she prepared us a meal.

Here Frank Dufresne, a member of our party, and I were afflicted with snow blindness. The next day, when our guides started back for the Yukon, the rest of our permanent party traveled on to the schoolhouse at the Eskimo village at Hooper Bay, but Frank and I lay in the darkness in the attic of that cabin, nursing our snow-blind eyes. The Eskimo woman crouched on the floor below, muttering guttural soliloquies by the hour, but three times a day she set before us boiled meat or hash and potatoes. Frank and I were more than thankful when we were recovered enough so we could take the remaining team and go over to join our party at Hooper Bay.

Our expedition to the Hooper Bay region was by no means all misery. I tell this part of it to show what difficulties we encounter at times in the north. But spring and fine weather were on their way, and many birds arrived to nest all through that area. All was well in our work; we had an outstandingly enjoyable season.

One of those fine days I stood on a grassy knoll overlooking the ice-littered shore of the Bering Sea. To the north a low mountain range, cobalt blue in the balmy air of spring, nosed out to sea, forming a prominent cape. Farther north, far beyond the range of vision, I knew the Yukon was emptying its turbid water. To the south, the flat coastline faded away in distance, and somewhere in the southwest, beyond the horizon, lay the Aleutian Islands. A jumble of twittering, tinkling, happy notes came from the air behind me. I turned to see a little bird fluttering in the ecstasy of his love song—the Alaska longspur, John Burroughs' "bobolink of the North." Beyond him lay the tundra.

A prophetic elation stirred me as I surveyed the awakening landscape. Under the onslaught of the returning sun, the snow was melting fast. Forgotten were the wintry plains, the biting, sweeping winds and drifting snow. After the strenuous winter the malamutes were resting, the dogsleds put away. Among the scattered ice pans I saw Eskimos putting out in kayaks after seals.

The tundra in spring! Hordes of birds were returning from the south, and the tundra resounded with their songs and trills, their quacking, booming, hooting, chirping—each after its kind giving voice to its exuberance. Yet some, such as the resplendent Steller's eiders, I never heard.

Why, among the lively host of tundra birds, should the Steller's eider so cling in my memory? There was the great snowy owl, with his family of gray, roly-poly owlets; the emperor goose; rare little shorebirds—a brilliant array of avian personalities. Many of these deserve more than passing notice, yet there was something friendly about the little eider. Perhaps something of the lure of the Arctic, the sunset over the tundra, colors my estimate of this little bird. After all, the eider is a part of the North.

As the season grew I made many new acquaintances among the Arctic avifauna. I had marveled at the tremendous migration of king eiders that passed on their way to the Arctic coast. The great Pacific eiders appeared, too, flock after flock, in endless numbers. Steller's eiders came in a less spectacular manner, yet I soon became aware of their presence among the shallow lakes of the tundra and tidal marshes. Smallest of the eiders, they are the most charming.

They enjoyed gathering on the shores of tidewater ponds to preen and visit together—a delightful array of shining plumage and varied colors. The little drakes glory in a raiment of steely blue back and buff waistcoat, merging into a rich, dark brown below, with white-striped scapulars drooping gracefully over white-shouldered wings. The white head is adorned with the usual touch of eider green. As though this were not enough, they have a black beauty spot in the buff near the shoulder, and a black chin and eye-ring. The females, as usual with the eiders, are dressed in modest brown. But in a mixed flock, the males are bright enough to throw a colorful glamor over the whole company.

As the season wore on, I learned to know these birds more intimately. I was tramping over the tundra with two Eskimo boys one day in July, after the fervor of early spring was gone. No longer could I hear the hubbub of mating song, except for the occasional flight song of a Wilson snipe. In the grass, among the knolls, and along the grassy margins of ponds—in many a secret nook lay hidden birds, quietly incubating eggs. The sharp eyes of an Eskimo boy spied one of these, a female Steller's eider on the nest. I took out my camera, a necessary burden for portraying the wildlife of the tundra. The eider proved to be a good "sitter." Slowly, as I moved up inch by inch, the image grew on the ground glass of my Graflex. But a clump of grass partly concealed her bill. I mentioned this fact in a low undertone to the Eskimo boys. One of them crept up, nearer and nearer, until he actually reached out and pressed down the offending grass, within an inch of the duck's head! Moreover, he reached back and removed some more obstructions by her side. Then, carefully, he retreated, and I took the photograph. This Eskimo youth knew eider nature better than I did.

Careless maneuvering on our part finally drove the bird off the nest, and she fled to a little pond nearby. There, to my surprise, she was joined by her mate. Where had he come from? It is customary for the males to return to carefree bachelorhood when incubation is well under way. Later experience taught me that the Steller husband is really quite devoted, lingering in the vicinity of the nest unusually long. Finally we went away, leaving the anxious pair swimming side by side in the little pond.

Eider devotion was brought home to me more forcibly on another occasion. I found a Steller's eider on her nest near the shore of a small pond. Instinctively, I unslung my camera and proceeded with the usual photography. It was not a difficult subject, and I soon had all the desired exposures, at very close range. Eventually, I crowded a little too close, and the bird left her nest and retreated to the pond. Then I saw that several eggs were pipped and about to hatch.

The mother's anxiety was pitiful. She swam to and fro, uttering a low *uhrrr, uhrrr.* When a little one within the eggshell peeped, she would hear its voice and come headlong for the nest—but she retreated again in the face of the great, camera-laden human hulk. I could bring her within close camera range by faintly peeping like one of her babies. To complicate matters, a rain shower came up. Then did the little mother show her sturdy spirit. Here was a new danger, more imminent than the other, one which touched her mother's instinct to the quick. Despite the giant enemy towering above her eggs, she climbed out on the bank, deliberately walked to the nest, and carefully tucked in her treasures! She pulled down and straw from the rim of the nest over the eggs, until she was satisfied the rain could do no harm. Only one egg was still visible under the downy blanket. Unmindful of my presence and the clicking of the camera scarcely five feet away, she busied herself at the nest. Then she walked back to the pond and swam about, watching me as before. I withdrew as quickly and quietly as I could.

On another day I was traveling with a companion, laden with the inevitable camera, when we spied a spectacled eider on her nest. This species is somewhat larger than Steller's eider, but the male is just as flashily dressed. He wears a circular patch of velvety blue feathers around each eye, producing a ludicrous appearance of spectacles. The female, of course, is a drab brown, but even she has a pair of lighter brown "spectacles."

There she lay, comfortably settled on her nestful of eggs, only a few feet from where we stood. The eiders are faithful brooders, and this one did not stir as we set up our tripod and made several time exposures. We watched her for a time, admiring her steadfastness, but eventually we came a little too near. She fluttered off the nest and fled to a nearby pond. We had the pictures we desired, so we slung the camera equipment on our backs and walked away.

But we had not gone far when, looking back, we saw a pomarine jaeger drawing near. The disturbance at the nest had attracted the attention of this gull-like hunter, and he was here to investigate. The jaeger resembles the seagull that nests in the same area, but is much darker, appearing almost black above, with a more hooked beak and sharper claws. Indeed, some jaegers have a habit of robbing the seagull of its food, just as the bald eagle takes the hard-earned fish from the osprey.

The jaeger soon spied the nestful of eggs, hovered over the spot for a few moments, then began fluttering downward. We were responsible for the jaeger's opportunity, but we were already too far away to avert the impending tragedy. Breathlessly and guiltily we watched the ominous, fluttering descent of that bird for its final pounce on those eggs.

But we had not reckoned with maternal instinct. From the little pond came a splashing sound, and a brown bird hurtled low over the ground with desperately beating wings. Straight for the nest flew the mother eider, and just as the jaeger was about to drop, she adroitly slid beneath him and covered her treasures. We watched the frustrated jaeger flutter about uncertainly for a while and finally drift away to other hunting grounds. We left the mother to exult in her victory. When next she left her nest, there would be a protective downy coverlet, both to keep the eggs warm and to hide them from prying eyes.

In the early spring, among the hosts of migrant shorebirds, there had come a little fellow who gave vent to his exuberance in a strange manner. No trilling song had he for mating time, but as he flew he puffed out the loose skin on his throat into a great pendant pouch, from which came a booming sound, *oomp, oomp, oomp, oomp* . . . we would see him beating in steady flight over the tundra. This was the pectoral sandpiper. The Eskimos called him tum-tum-tak, referring to his booming courtship flight. No doubt this performance seemed eminently suitable to the brown female hidden somewhere in the grass.

When egg-laying began, these proved to be wary birds. For a time I despaired of even finding a nest, since the female would slip off it while I was still at a great distance. Certainly I did not expect to come to any intimate terms with this cautious mother.

Then came the time when the brooding birds began to be rewarded by fuzzy, animated little creatures emerging from those long-guarded eggs. I was out with an Eskimo boy when we came upon a newly hatched brood of four little pectoral sandpipers. We admired the rich chestnut of their mottled downy suits and took them in our hands to fondle them. What about their mother? There she came, and the camera clicked, but still she came— excited, scolding, drawing nearer and nearer. She had been shy and secretive about her eggs, but not so with her babies in danger.

She was now so near that I had an idea for a picture. Instructing the Eskimo boy to crouch low to the ground with the little ones in his hands, I backed off a little with the camera. Here she came—the camera clicked again, but still she came. Then, to our astonishment, she actually went up to the Eskimo's fingers and attempted to "hover" her chicks! She even managed to fluff her feathers protectingly over one of the chicks while the boy still held it by the feet!

There were brave mothers aplenty on these prolific nesting grounds— bold ones, who would threaten and bluff; meek ones, who would quietly cling to their brood in the face of danger, hoping the intruder would pass by; and clever ones, who would sight danger afar and discreetly withdraw from their nests in order not to betray their locations. Each behaved in accordance with her own accomplishments and peculiar nature. Mothers all, they lived their lives as nature had decreed. *Tum-tum-tak*, the shy one, climbed into the Eskimo's hand to hover her chicks; *kow-wuk*, the spectacled one, braved the hook-beaked jaeger for her family. And my thoughts return to the plucky eider who came to my very feet to tuck in her babies. I think of her returning to her nest after my departure, pulling aside the downy coverlet, fondly billing the eggs a moment, then snuggling down among them, a crooning eider sound in her throat.

I hope she raised her family. I hope every spring the tundra ponds are graced by these little folk, for the fulfillment of their own destiny and the enrichment of man's spirit.

This page intentionally left blank

ALASKA: THE LATER YEARS

Exploring the Brooks Range

Our little plane slanted down and landed on the ice of a lake. Over on the shore were the tents put up the day before by the two young men of our expedition, who came running out over the ice to meet us. This was June 1, 1956. All five of us gathered there and watched the plane go off into the south; then we carried our gear over to the shore. We were on our own.

And why were we here? We pondered that question often as the weeks of summer went by. It was one of those missions that cannot be readily explained. Briefly, the New York Zoological Society, the Conservation Foundation, and The Wilderness Society, being much interested in preserving the intangible values of the Arctic, had sent us up here to look into the character of the Brooks Range.

Here we were, in camp beside an unnamed lake, more than 150 miles north of the Arctic Circle. Perhaps George Schaller expressed the spirit of the place that first day when he met us out on the lake ice: "This is a wonderful place. I want to *stay* up here!"

Why? That is what we were to try to find out. We sat at the campfire that evening and looked out over that northland. On both sides rose the rugged mountains, and we all looked forward to exploring up there. There was the big valley between, in which we had our camp, and to the south stretched the lowland to the far horizon.

As we sat there, two grizzlies appeared across the river. In front of us, a muskrat was swimming about in the open water near shore. We had already seen certain gulls and ducks on their way to northern nesting places. What were we thinking, each one of us? George Schaller had already expressed his outlook when he so enthusiastically greeted us out there on the lake. Bob Krear didn't say much but I felt that he didn't need to put it into words. He is a mountain climber, skier, outdoorsman—an able wilderness traveler. Brina Kessel was a young professor of zoology at the University of Alaska, who was sent on the expedition to see what she could learn about the zoological significance of this bit of country. As for my wife, Mardy, and me, we had both been in many parts of Alaska in previous years. But here we were, on a new adventure. What about it?

I had given this venture much thought. Here was a part of the North at stake—a symbol of the whole circumpolar Arctic. What should mankind do with it? A few brilliant scientists discover important laws; the rest of us enthusiastically apply those findings in thousands of ways. But in our enthusiasm we tend to forget the fundamental aspects of nature as presented to us on this planet. Will we have the patience to observe and try to understand what the northern part of the earth has to offer?

We discussed, vaguely, what we had before us. All I could say to those young people was, "The success of this expedition must be measured by what each one of us gets out of his experience up here."

In the following days we all wandered eagerly over the country—in the valley, on the mountain slopes—going singly or in pairs, in all directions. Those grizzlies we saw on the first day were a preview of many later experiences. Everywhere we saw signs of grizzlies—tracks on the sandbars, moss and turf torn up in places where the bears had been digging for roots, piles of rock and earth where they had dug out ground squirrels. Once we found a hibernation den on a mountainside. And occasionally we saw the bears themselves.

On the sandbars we also saw tracks of wolves. One day a wolf came over the rise back of camp and seemed surprised to see us there—invaders of his wild-country home! We looked at him, thrilled by this close view of an animal that seemed to represent the wilderness and freedom of this far land. We gazed silently at each other. Then he went on to the lake ice and trotted across to the far shore. We were all so moved by this silent interview with a striking creature of the wild that by common consent we called this lake "Lobo Lake" in honor of our visitor.

As we wandered through the valley and over the mountains, we came upon little groups of caribou. On one occasion, on a mountainside east of camp, we saw a band of them traveling through scattered spruce trees. Another time we came within very close camera range of a half dozen of them on a slope above a pond. Again, we watched a group coming down the open bars of a stream, where we were hidden on the bank. Alert, looking for danger? Yes, to be sure. But we felt that they enjoyed living here, traveling up and down stream bars, over the tundra, and on the mountain slopes. They harmonized so perfectly with the landscape—they belonged here.

Each day in the wilderness holds something of interest, and we found the long days of June in Arctic Alaska brimful of interest and little adventures. Several times, bands of caribou crossed the ice in front of camp, and each time our cameras and my sketchbook were put to use.

The snow was gone from the land, and flowers were beginning to appear. The caribou—and we too—used the lake ice to walk on as long as possible, but the ice was thawing around the edges, and it became a tricky problem to cross over. This was the state of affairs on the 6th of June. Mardy's journal of the following day speaks of what happened:

"Yesterday morning's breakfast was enlivened by a different kind of Ice Follies, by a troupe of 28 caribou. I had the first 3 pancakes in the skillet and happened to glance toward the east end of Lobo Lake. 'Here they come! Here they come!'

"Bob dove for the movie-, George and Olaus for their still cameras. Brina, dishing up prunes, said 'I just refuse to use up any more film on caribou on ice!'

" 'Well, I might as well postpone the pancake baking till they get by' and I covered the 3 cakes and set the skillet off the flame."

There they came, led by a bull. At least thirteen were plainly adult bulls, with antlers in the velvet. Possibly they were all bulls, of various ages. As they came opposite us, they spied our camp; perhaps they heard the clicking of cameras, for they broke into a trot until they were well past us. We watched them with our glasses as they approached the west shore. There they stopped, for they knew the shore ice was treacherous. Then began a long period of making up their caribou minds; we at camp were the fascinated spectators. They had crossed the lake for the good walking, but now they wanted to get up onto the land. But how? There was that treacherous thawing ice, and the little strip of water. Two or three started slowly in our direction, and the others fell in behind—but only for a little way. Then the leaders turned around and went back, the others following. Another started off bravely, and the band followed, but the same thing happened—back to the starting point. The band continued to get nowhere.

As Mardy spoke of it in her journal: "They came by, led by a bull, and went on past to the west end—stopped, stood, turned, and traveled toward the north end, stopped, stood, milled around, came back a way, stood. This kind of thing went on for at least thirty minutes. We went ahead and cooked and ate, watching the while, everyone making comments on indecision, mass psychology, Congress, the U.N., and human politics in general, of which this scene reminded us."

We were amused and fascinated, guessing at the outcome of that spectacle of indecision out there on the ice. Time and again one or two would start off in a certain direction, as if those individuals were thinking, in caribou language, "By gum! Somethin's got to be done!"

But each time those leaders seemed to realize that they were out in front and didn't want so much responsibility. So they would turn around and lead the rest back to the assembly place. Then they would wait for someone else to have a thought.

There came a slight break in the monotony. Over a rise in the land beyond the lake to the west came a lone bull. He saw the band of his fellows and came eagerly to join them. Without hesitation he crossed over onto the ice and joined the crowd.

How can one judge exactly what is in the mind of another person, let alone the mind of a caribou? We must interpret action in the light of human experience, observation, and reasoning about life in general. Would we be wrong in reasoning that the caribou is a herd animal, used to being in companies or even great herds, and that as a consequence, the individuals depend on the mass? The lone caribou came upon this band and had the impulse to join it. He could not depend on anyone else—the initiative was obviously his alone—and he went over onto the ice.

As we sat there eating our breakfast in camp, the indecision continued. One of them started back across the lake, where they had come from. But I suppose the far shore suddenly seemed a long way off, for they turned back, and there was a lot of milling about this time. Perhaps there had been a vague feeling that back there across the lake was not where they had started out to go. As the herd stood there, incapable of decision, one of them lay down on the ice. Might as well rest until someone makes up his mind! Another followed his example. At one time there were four lying there, placidly waiting until "they" would do something.

This was an exhibition of mass behavior, human or otherwise, being played before us there on Lobo Lake as on a stage. The moose is a very different sort of animal, meeting the exigencies of life alone or in small groups. A few days earlier we had seen a moose near the Sheenjek River, and from what we had seen, the moose had more self-reliance, more determination. In the situation before us, we felt that a lone moose would have done something promptly, though of course that was speculation.

As we watched, a caribou bull started off, and the whole herd followed. Those lying down got up, so as not to be left behind—maybe "they" were going somewhere at last! But the leaders lost their courage again and back they came. By this time we were very conscious of a caribou problem, minor in its way, but perhaps significant if we could only interpret what we saw.

Then, at last, it happened. A single caribou had the gumption to cross over to the land, jumping the gap and splashing to shore. Was it that lone bull who had joined the band late? We could only wonder. But anyway one animal braved the treacherous ice and sloshed through water to the dry ground.

The spell was broken; "the die was cast." One by one the whole herd followed, meekly, trustingly. Soon they were all feeding contentedly on the tundra.

Leadership!

IN LATE JUNE, PILOT KEITH HARRINGTON CAME AGAIN WITH THE LITTLE bush plane and moved us upriver to a smaller lake farther into the mountains, which we called Last Lake. It was the most northerly lake in the Sheenjek valley. From the valley we had gone out in many directions. We had climbed mountains, gone up through passes, found little lakes and streams, discovered bird nests on the ground, in bushes, and on cliffs, and seen many kinds of flowers—a rich and full life.

But the mountains to the north, toward the head of the Sheenjek River, kept beckoning. We were not satisfied; we always wanted to see and discover more in this land of far places. So on July 20 Mardy and I each put in a packsack some food, a sleeping bag, and a piece of cheesecloth to keep off mosquitoes at night. We packed one air mattress to spread beneath both sleeping bags. Thus equipped, we started up the valley in perfectly clear weather. Oh, yes, we had our notebooks, field glasses, and camera! How could we go anywhere without them?

By that time the overflow ice fields were disintegrating here and there, had become treacherous underfoot. Earlier in the summer, when they were firm, they had provided us with excellent walking, and we could appreciate why the caribou preferred to walk on the ice. For a distance on this first day upriver we did find a trail of a sort along the river. But then I undertook to make a shortcut across a tussocky tundra flat. I think that proved to be the hardest walking I had ever encountered. At times one of us would fall down, then the other, as we staggered along on tricky, irregular footing through that sea of tussocks—it can hardly be described.

Earlier, we had come upon a bull caribou near a thawing overflow ice field, and he had run up the valley. Here we came on him again, in this tussock area. He ran easily across the valley in front of us until he disappeared in a distant patch of woods. I shall not forget Mardy's envious comment as we watched the disappearing caribou: "If only we could trot across the country as easily as that!"

We were so tired by the time we reached a little pass at the head of the tussock sea that we camped there by a rocky outcrop. We spread our bags, made a fire of dry willow limbs, and had our supper, finding water in a little, mossy pool.

It was good to crawl into the sleeping bags after supper. It was a cold night, though never dark; in the morning, we were cold and found thick ice on the little pans of water. We were looking eagerly for the sun to peep over the top of the high mountains just above us. Then it came, in a clear sky, and it seemed to say, "Here I am! Now everything will be fine!"

And it was. I built a fire of dry willows, and we had breakfast. I thawed out my frozen rubber pacs and put them on; we thawed the frost off our sleeping bags, and in a few moments could forget the cold night of troubled sleep and look out on a wonderful new day.

We traveled up the valley, following the river at times. On some of the sandy bars we saw the tracks of wolves and grizzly bears. Here and there a red fox had left his sign, and we found where a porcupine had crossed the sand. And there were birds—the willow ptarmigan as always, and trim little semipalmated plovers on the river bars. We also saw a Bohemian waxwing and a shrike, both to be expected in this north country.

We shall always remember our last camp up the river. We made it in the lee of a clump of willows in a sandy-gravelly place, with a little stream trickling by to join the Sheenjek beyond. While I was taking some pictures, Mardy picked a place for our beds on the gravel bar. She gathered some willows for a pillow and laid our one air mattress crosswise. We placed two little rocks a short distance apart to hold our one kettle, over a fire of willow sticks, and soon our simple supper was underway.

There is something exhilarating about making a simple wilderness camp. All we had were the beds—no tents—and the little campfire. Even so, for us it was comparable to building a home, and it really was our home for a few days.

The next day was our last day northward, our farthest north on this expedition. Sometimes you have an experience that you cannot adequately describe; this was one of them. First, we had a wonderful sleep at our little camp. Then I got up early, feeling fit for our last day up the Sheenjek. I went up a side valley to photograph some cottongrass I had seen up there, before the wind should come up. But by the time I got there, the sun had gone behind a mountain on its way upward. I could see the early morning sunlight on mountain slopes down the valley, but the flowers and I stood in the shadow, waiting. It was not long. I picked out some good positions from which to photograph the blossoms, with distant mountains in the background. Soon the life-giving sun peeped over the mountain, and in a few minutes the plants and I were in a flood of sunshine. The cottongrass, with its fluffy white pompons in a cluster at the water's edge or dotting a green meadow, always made me stop to admire this bit of beauty so characteristic of the North.

At camp Mardy had a good breakfast of mush and stewed fruit ready. Then we put some lunch in my packsack and started off for the day.

First, we had to cross the river. Here it was shallow and broken up into many channels; we waded across easily, and though we got our feet a bit wet, that didn't bother us; we were used to it.

As we came over to a steep mountain slope on the other side, we saw trails up above leading from one patch of green vegetation to another. Had mountain sheep been there, or caribou? This was new country to us, and we wanted to know.

"Well, I guess the best way to make sure is to go up there, rather than to go on speculating. Mardy, suppose you explore around on this country ahead of us while I go up there."

"All right. I'll be just ahead here."

Wherever we went in this country, there was something to see and wonder about. There were so many little things on that climb up to those trails. There were the plants growing there; what kind were they, and why were they so scattered, in clumps? Of course, this was near the limit of plant growth on this bare rocky slope. I did explore those trails and found the skull of a caribou. I concluded that there had been no mountain sheep to make the trails—only caribou.

As Mardy and I went on along the slopes above the river, we saw a wheatear on a hummock, the first we had seen up here, and pipits also—true northern birds. We found another caribou trail, a well-trodden way to go up to higher ground. Soon we were traveling well above the valley bottom; we had a good view of the open country below us, the river being over on the north side. The trail we were on was obviously made entirely by caribou. Was this a regular migration route? It added to our adventurous feeling to be sharing the route of a wild animal. We had chosen to go up along here, and so had they.

Then something startling came to our attention—not a dramatic occurrence but a normal thing which still caused us surprise. Going along the caribou trail, we came to a place where very large willows were scattered along, just below us. A swallow shot past, too fast for us to have a good look. We had seen cliff swallows downriver, but this one seemed smaller. Then it came back, and there was another one. They began zigzagging in the air in a fashion that made it a real game to get the field glasses on them. But now I had a suspicion. I asked Mardy, who has a keen eye for color, "Did you see any green on the back?"

"Yes, a beautiful violet and green!"

She had glimpsed these colors with the naked eye. As I had suspected, these were violet-green swallows, the first we had seen in the Brooks Range. I recalled that I had first seen them years ago in Oregon and had become familiar with them among the cliffs in Jackson Hole, Wyoming. Here they were, near the head of the Sheenjek River in the Brooks Range of the Alaskan Arctic, far north of the Arctic Circle! Life does get around on this planet!

Farther up the valley we came to great outwash alluvial fans, coming out of small rocky canyons at our left. Here the trail we were following sprayed out in various directions across this smooth, well-vegetated area. The valley was still quite wide here, with the main channel of the river far across on the opposite side.

We came to a high point on one of those alluvial fans and there before us, high on the mountain terrain in the north, was a small, white glacier. Here was the beginning of our river! We were beyond the limit of trees, and over there was the summit of the Brooks Range.

We spent some time on that hilltop, having our lunch and exploring around nearby. We found ground squirrel burrows and examined a mound where an owl evidently was in the habit of sitting to enjoy a meal. Was it the white owl, the *okpik* of the Eskimo? We thought it must be.

There is always a "going back," and finally, reluctantly, we turned southward. In late afternoon, as we again picked up the caribou trail, we came again to the swallows. This time we saw some immature birds on the wing. Some lit for a while on willows below us, and several times an adult flew up to feed a young one. There was a great flutter of wings by both—the young to beg and the adult to keep itself in the air.

Such an aerial display! How these birds could cut through the air! And almost as fast as the eye could follow, they would be shooting back in the other direction—up and down and off, in a wonderful pattern of flight. I think it was so impressive to us because we ourselves were high on a caribou trail on a mountain slope, far above the stream. So our minds could the more easily share the air experience of the swallows. Just above us were some cliffs where they evidently had found crevices for their nests.

Next morning we headed back southward toward base camp at Last Lake; it would take two days of travel in this land of midnight sunlight, two days full of poignant little adventures. We saw no more swallows on the way back. We traveled well out in the middle of the valley on the gravel bars of the river, carefully avoiding the sea of tussocks through which we had struggled on the upriver trip. One of our little adventures was watching a semipalmated plover out on one of the bars, a mature bird with a downy young. They both ran off over the gravel; they were the same shades of gray and black as the gravel. Farther along we passed a wide meadow covered solidly with mountain avens, now all converted to silken, silvery seed heads.

At our last camp on the way back, we spread our sleeping bags on the bank of the main river, in the edge of a long grove of spruce. And from our beds we watched an unforgettable scene as the sun moved across a gap in the mountains, casting a red-gold reflection in the water of the Sheenjek. I do not recall what dreams we had that night, but since then there have been many daytime dreams about our wilderness travels in that land of the midnight sun in Arctic Alaska.

Flowers on Ice

In June Dr. Donald MacLeod flew up from Jackson Hole, Wyoming, to join our party for a brief vacation in the Arctic. One day, he, Bob Krear, and I climbed to the top of the highest mountain near our camp. On the way up, I kept going off in several directions, following caribou tracks, trying to see what they were doing up here in high country. Finally, we assembled at the top, and there we saw their tracks again, far above any vestige of plant growth. What were they doing up here? I remembered that many years ago Theodore Roosevelt had written that often a bull elk would go out on a mountain point, as if he simply enjoyed the scenery.

As we sat there on the mountain, enjoying just *being there*, I pondered the outlook of those caribou. They could have crossed at a low pass. Why did they come up on this high mountain, where there was no food for them? Earlier, we had seen a golden eagle fly in among the cliffs of another mountain. Of course, these creatures—the eagle and this remarkable circumpolar deer called caribou or reindeer—presumably do not define their feelings to themselves! But can we not venture to think that they *like* things—that going places means something to them? The birds we saw, and the caribou, bear, wolf, and so many other natural manifestations gave life to this land. They inspired us to go places, to see, to appreciate, and to try to understand.

Not the least part of our experience was what we found among the flowers. When we first came to Lobo Lake, we landed on the ice; but other lakes, for some reason, were ice-free, and the land was bare of snow. In a few days George Schaller made a trip into the mountains and found alpine flowers already in bloom on some of the high slopes. But the high point of the whole floristic display was the profusion of rhododendron on the lower slopes bordering the whole valley. They came into bloom about the middle of June and gave a lovely pinkish tone to the slopes behind our camp. And with them were the deep blue lupine and the white mountain avens, *Dryas octopetala*.

These rhododendrons made me think of the rhododendrons on the other side of the world in the Himalayas, where many colorful pheasants live, as is so vividly told by William Beebe in his great work on the pheasants of the world. Here in the American Arctic lives a relative of the pheasants, the ptarmigan, which has adapted itself to living in snow country, as have so many other birds, mammals, and flowers. The ptarmigan seemed to be everywhere. In the flat tundra formation, among the tussocks, were many flowers, including certain attractive little plants growing humbly among the sedges and mosses. These were the bright purple *Pedicularis*, called, for some reason, lousewort. Each plant had a single flower, a thick spike composed of many flowerets. A little higher on the slopes, among other flowers, we especially enjoyed the arctic poppy; and in midsummer appeared the tall, showy boykenia with its creamy white stalk of flowers. In the mountain passes and on lower hillsides, these became a feature of the landscape. It was pleasant to look over a smooth slope and see spikes of these boykenia flowers rising here and there above the mat of lower plant growth.

In the mountains were whole cliff ledges crowded with mats of creamy saxifrage, and I liked to look past these flowering ledges to the Arctic mountain landscape beyond.

Such a surprising flora of adventurous flowers, pushing blithely and confidently northward and upward, as far as any accumulation of soil permitted them to put in their roots! We were intrigued by the great variety of colorful lichens and mosses, those primitive members of the plant world that thrive on the bare rocks and sparse soil. In some places, brightly colored lichens—red, yellow, and blue—decorated prominent rocks in the landscape. And we found charming mossy areas along streams or pools that furnished an ideal environment.

Then we were made aware of Arctic phenomena that have a bearing on the flora of the region. One of these is permafrost—over large areas, the soil is permanently frozen. In some places we found pure ice underground. I suppose this fact, along with the ice of the polar seas, has given rise to the common idea of the "frozen wasteland of the Arctic." But permafrost needs more explanation.

We found that near the surface there is a layer of moss and other vegetation, with a little thawed soil. But down beneath this, the ground is permanently frozen. In much of Arctic Alaska, for example, the annual precipitation has been given as about eight inches, which in a temperate climate such as Arizona would be considered desert. But the ice of the frozen ground gives off enough surface moisture to support a flourishing, varied flora. Everywhere we went, we found puddles and ponds of water—wetness everywhere in the valley. So over large areas, the Arctic flowers literally grow on ice! And what a lovely variety of blooms we have there, little and big. We can get the full appreciation of all this if we enter the Arctic humbly, with an inquiring mind, and look for the modest beauty to be found all about us.

The permafrost is scattered irregularly—not all the north has it—and the edges of the affected area are variable. The map shows its approximate location about the polar regions.

We found other strong evidences of a bygone age. In several places a steep bank had sloughed away, exposing a layer of pure ice. In some cases

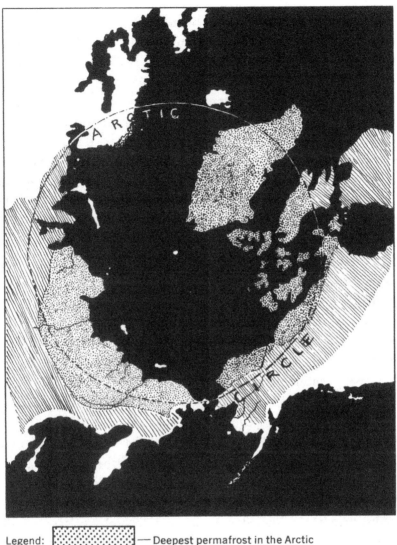

Legend:

▦ —Deepest permafrost in the Arctic

▨ —Shallower, irregular permafrost

PERMAFROST AREAS OF THE ARCTIC

Map by Olaus Murie. The original bore his longhand notation: "Permafrost occurs here and there farther south, but we do not have it all mapped yet."

there was a foot or more of soil over the ice. These were obviously ancient frozen ponds that had become covered with cold earth. They were hidden underground all those centuries until the bank, made steep by erosion, slid away to expose this cross-section of ice to our view.

In 1926 Mardy and I and our ten-month-old son, with our friend Jesse Rust, traveled by motorboat to the headwaters of the Old Crow River in Yukon Territory. Our mission was to band young geese in order to learn their migration routes. As we worked up the river, we passed many high, steep bluffs of mud, which were actively being sloughed away. The whole Old Crow River area had been a Pleistocene lake bottom, and the high bluffs we traveled along were remnants of the steep banks of that ancient lake. In these banks, often far down from the top, lenses of ice were exposed. We liked to think of them as old "fossil ponds." In the same banks we found bones and tusks of mammoth, teeth and bones of bison and horses, and one tooth of the giant beaver. On the river bars we would occasionally see a black bear feeding on the abundant horsetail, or a caribou, or a peregrine falcon nesting on the bluffs. What a place to be in! All the present-day animals were well adapted to this northern habitat—an adaptation that had taken so many centuries that they all felt this was their ancestral home. But unknown to them, there was clear evidence of other great animals that at one time lived here and looked upon this as *their* home. But those animals are gone now, and the Pleistocene lake is now flat tundra with a winding river that we newcomers call "Old Crow!" Things do change—all of them.

During our 1956 expedition to the Sheenjek River valley, we found that the extensive areas of ice adjacent to the stream lasted into the first part of August before they thawed away in the perpetual summer sun. Thus, when the flowers bloomed on the mountain slopes and ice-free parts of the valley, and when birds raised their young in the warm summer season with its midnight sunshine, the overflow ice served as a constant reminder of the long, sunless winter.

However, the flowers crowded hard upon this ice. On the higher ground they bloomed, had their growth, and went to seed in June and July. Those plants under the ice had to wait. Then, as the ice melted away, flowers would come up in the newly released earth. Late in summer some of these were bravely in bloom, when those of the same species on higher ground had bloomed long ago and were now in seed!

Thus we could see the resilience of both plant and animal life in the north country—how it takes every little advantage to flourish and produce offspring.

One morning early in June I lay in the tent, the sun shining dimly through the canvas; I turned my face into the sleeping bag to shut out the light. Outside I could hear the male ptarmigan talking. At this time of year they are conspicuous with their brown necks and white bodies, crowing and "talking"—they seem to dominate the tundra landscape. I could lie in the tent listening to them and visualize the wide, open expanse of country, with the ptarmigan bubbling his spring fervor in his guttural way. I could hear the small trill of the tree sparrow, enjoying the same thing in a more modest way. I knew the muskrat would be swimming about in the water along the lakeshore, busy with his little affairs, whatever they might be. And out there, somewhere, the bands of caribou were going their silent way. What a peaceful, beautiful world!

MAY 27, 1961. AGAIN VETERAN PILOT KEITH HARRINGTON, SO APPRECIA-tive of nature's beauty, took us north of Fort Yukon in the little plane of the Wien-Alaska Airlines. He flew low over the flat country, north toward the mountains, and landed us once more on the ice of Lobo Lake. We managed to get ashore, although the ice was melting around the edges. Keith helped us carry our gear up to the old camp before he flew off into the south.

Mardy and I were on our own this time, five years later. We had to come back to the Arctic! We quickly put up our camp. Trees were sparse here and we would not cut any, but one of our tents had a metal pole, and we found enough dry fallen trees for the other. We had the Coleman gas stove to cook on.

Again early spring was coming to the northland; waterbirds and land birds were already here in numbers. And already there were flowers, even in these last days of May. Pussy willows were out in all their gaiety, and we found one of the very first flowers—*Saxifraga oppositifolia*, bright little red-purple flowers growing close to the ground. As soon as camp was set up we climbed to our old favorite spot on the ridge above. There on the northern tip of the ridge, looking up the Sheenjek valley to the north, we found a male ptarmigan sitting among deep blue blossoms of pasque flowers of some kind. Out on the tundra the tussocks were beginning to bloom.

As the first few days went by, I kept thinking about why we two had come back up here. We were both accustomed to living in the northland, and I suppose much of our lives is influenced by environment. But there must be an attitude inherent in us that strives for expression. And I think there is another deep-seated impulse—one that is emerging throughout the world—to try to improve our culture. There is in all of us the urge to share beauty and freedom with other sensitive people.

These thoughts came to me as Mardy and I sat on the hill near the ptarmigan, looking at the winding Sheenjek River below, the distant snow-streaked mountains, and the clouds overhead. We again listened to the guttural crowing of the ptarmigan and the calling of many other birds—old familiar friends. Freedom, in all directions, to the horizon and beyond! Yes, we felt strongly that we wanted to share all this with the birds, the wandering caribou, and with other people.

Later in the season we had just that opportunity. First, Keith brought in our friend Charlotte Mauk from California for a ten-day visit. Later, two fifteen-year-old boys came, all the way from Washington, D.C. All three of these visitors were sensitive people with the honest urge to explore, to enjoy, and to record with their cameras. They all seemed to have a wonderful time, and it gave us deep satisfaction.

In that first week, while Mardy and I were alone in the country, we tried to take stock of our motives in coming back. Why do we do anything, anytime? All we knew was that it seemed good to us. Neither of us tried to put it into words. It was somehow like landing on a new planet—distance to the horizon and beyond, in all directions. The lake before us was ice-covered, but in the water near the shore waterbirds were already gathering, giving us the joy of recognizing one species after another. There were little

sprightly phalaropes, many other shorebirds, and ducks—our friends the old squaws and the baldpates. Soon we saw a pair of arctic loons. The whole land was awakening after the long, life-giving winter sleep.

One day we came on a clearly defined caribou track beside a clump of purple saxifrage. As we looked at the blooming flower and the track of that Arctic member of the deer clan, it occurred to us that here were a plant and an animal who had both found the Far North a fine place to live.

Back at camp we had some fresh meat we had brought along on the plane to start off our camp larder. Behind the tent we dug up a slab of mossy turf, put the wrapped meat down on the frozen ground, and put the turf back on top. That was our refrigerator—permafrost. That was what we had, and that was what all the plants had to live on. Could they exist together? We saw before our eyes abundant assurance that they could.

In the early part of our stay at Lobo Lake we had groups of anemones all around camp, and there were many little beds of them along the high bank of the Sheenjek. It made me remember that in Norway three years before, Mardy and I had come upon a mountain slope covered with anemones—they seemed to have taken over the whole mountainside.

I was in the tent writing notes when Mardy called to me from outside: "Just stick your head out!"

I crawled to the tent door and looked out. There, across the lake, against a dark cloud and beside a sunlit mountain, was a short, wide rainbow. And at that moment three old squaw ducks, calling in their loud goose-like voices, flew low over the ice-covered lake. They gave the true northern flavor to the scene.

The old squaws about the lake and the willow ptarmigan on the land enliven the north country with their calls at all times of day and night. Often at night I would lie in the tent listening to the voices of the land; all these, combined with the midnight sunlight, tended to keep one from sleeping.

On June 9 I walked all around Lobo Lake, but before I was very far from camp I heard Mardy calling. "What is it?" I yelled.

"Caribou!"

Then I saw them—our first band for this year. They were on my route around the lake, so I approached them carefully and got some pictures, then went on around the shore. Anemones were everywhere, on all suitable banks of the lake; during these few days they had suddenly come into bloom, as flowers do in the North. Here and there I also found the first modest *Pedicularis*, and farther on some *Pyrola*, or wintergreen. This plant is scarcer; I saw only a few. But the landscape as a whole had come to life. I should explain that the tundra itself—the flat part—consisted mostly of tussocks or sedges and cottongrass, with other plants here and there. But on the hills and ridges were often thickets of willow, dwarf birch, and a few alder bushes. On some of the hills it was hard to get through this brush. On this day around the lake, I saw whole slopes covered with moss, among the stems of shrubs and trunks of trees; that day there seemed to be moss everywhere I went. I took pleasure in the variety of lichens I found on rocks and old, dry trees. And whenever I went to the very shore of the lake, there were ducks—pintails, old squaws, scoters, and others—for by this time there was ice only in the middle of the lake.

Different flowers have different ways of living. I remember finding the *Cassiope* and the *Andromeda* (bog rosemary), which are rather similar. Each has small, drooping, bell-shaped flowers, whitish, which gave me the impression of nakedness. They grew humbly, and in some places I felt I was intruding where they were blooming. In many places I found the *Arctous*, a form of the bearberry, and of course there was the low, spreading crowberry, *Empetrum*, whose black berries last a good part of the winter. I must not forget to mention that here in the Sheenjek we also had the low blueberry and cranberry. The grizzly bear and other animals search out the blueberries when they finally ripen in August; the bear is especially fond of them.

On the hill back of camp, where the ptarmigan had sat, and we so often went, the *Dryas* bloomed a little later. In some places whole meadows were white with their blooms. At the same time, in mid-June, on all the slopes and in among the white *Dryas*, appeared the rosy bloom of the rhododendron—*Rhododendron lapponicum*, a widespread flower in the north country. It is circumpolar in distribution, but it seemed more abundant in the Sheenjek than any other Arctic valley we had known. On the hills all along the river the rhododendron's pink and the white of the *Dryas* mingled in great alpine gardens. How we gloried in it—how grateful we were to be there once more to enjoy this flowering.

In Scandinavia these flowers are also prominent in many places. But a rhododendron in the Arctic—that was a surprise to me when I first saw it years ago.

Another flower that caught my fancy was the large white pompon of the cottongrass. There are several kinds of *Eriophorum*, but one of them carries a prominent cluster of white. The blooms are like little tufts of cotton, each at the top of a grasslike stem. Whether you find a single cluster of them at the water's edge or a wide expanse dotting a wet meadow with white, they are a beautiful feature of the northland. Like many of the northern flowers, they are circumpolar.

I cannot, of course, name all the flowers. We often came on a little cushion of *Silene*, or moss campion—the little plant that puts out little pink flowers scattered thickly on a "cushion" of green mosslike growth. We found *Rumex* at the borders of ponds, and Indian paintbrush, *Senecio* (or groundsel), and rosy-pink rock fireweed.

One day I was walking along the shore of Lobo when I became aware of a group of lupine on a bank above the water. Here again was a flower growing in the foreground of a scene—the lake with phalaropes and ducks on its waters, backed by mountains and clouds.

This is not intended as a botanical review of the flora of the Brooks Range, or the Arctic in general. It is intended to show what you may find in the north country if you look for it. Part way up the mountain slopes there is greenery, but farther up, soil is just forming. And then you come to bare rock. In all this progress upward, you get a good view of the ecology of the North.

In December 1960, Secretary of the Interior Fred A. Seaton dedicated the northeastern corner of Alaska, including part of the Brooks Range, and all the territory we had explored, as the "Arctic National Wildlife Range." The idea, not yet understood by all, was to protect permanently another portion of our planet for sensitive people to go to get acquainted with themselves, to enjoy untouched nature, and to leave the lovely, unmarked country as they find it.

Beneath all those thriving blooms, all that Arctic beauty, is the solid frozen ground. In August autumn paints the blueberry bushes, cranberries, dwarf birch, and all the other growth, and the landscape takes on the colors appropriate for that season. If you can watch a caribou, or a grizzly, in the midst of that—what more do you want?

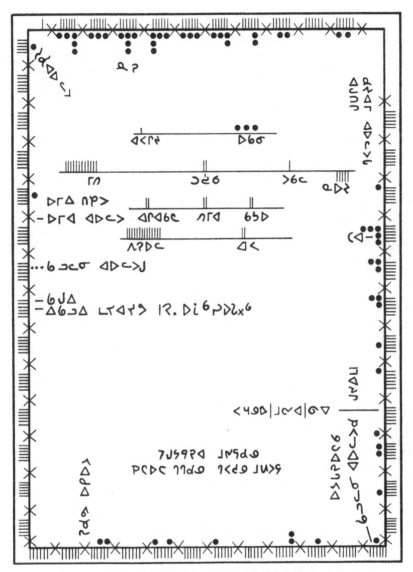

AN ESKIMO CALENDAR-DIARY

This is a diary of eight Eskimos in a seal-hunting camp. The heavy dots represent the number of seals killed on a particular day.

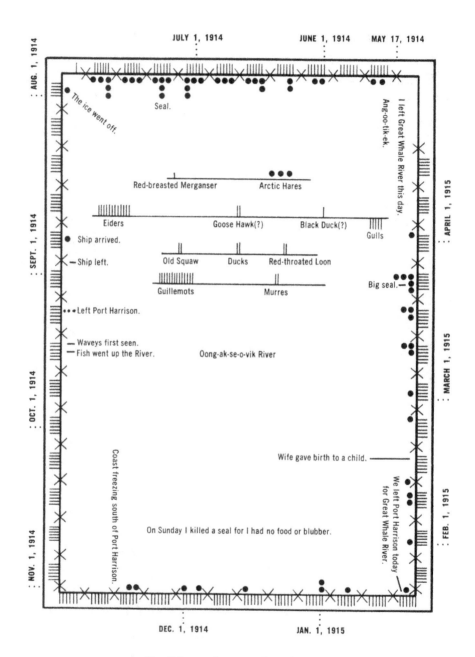

An English translation of the Eskimo diary

Olaus and his favorite sled dog, Jack.

*Indian lookout for spotting caribou herds, Dick Mitchell at top,
Upper Tanana River, Alaska, July 7, 1921.*

Olaus dancing with Aleut people of Nunivak Island, Alaska.

In the early years all of Olaus's winter travels in the Arctic were by dog team.

Angiok and his sister Mary, playing in a snow cave. (Courtesy of University of Alaska Archives)

Adolph steadies the sled as his dogs struggle up Eagle Summit.

Meal time at Last Lake camp. Mardy, Bob Krear, and Olaus. (Photo by George Schaller)

Dr. Brina Kessel and Olaus putting up specimens in camp. (Photo by Bob Krear)

Eagle nest cliff near Last Lake, looking north up the Sheenjek Valley.

Olaus packaging specimens, Sheenjek camp.

Peter Tritt, an Indian visitor, watches Olaus sketch. (Photo by George Schaller)

An able skier, mountain climber, and all-around outdoorsman, Bob Krear proved to be a pretty good barber as well. (Photo by George Schaller)

Olaus and Mardy leaving Last Lake for the head of the Sheenjek River.

George Schaller and ground squirrel size each other up. (Photo by Bob Krear)

This page intentionally left blank

PART II

OBSERVATIONS ON THE ARCTIC

This page intentionally left blank

THE LAND AND THE WILDLIFE

Where Is the Arctic?

We generally think of the "Arctic" as just up north somewhere and are inclined to shiver when we think of it. But there have been warmer times, even in what we think of now as the "Far North." For example, I have a fossil twig-tip of a redwood tree, similar to those wonderful big trees of coastal California. This fossil was found on St. Lawrence Island in Bering Sea, not far from the coast of Siberia. Today not a single tree grows there—it is in the Arctic—yet at one time the climate fostered a plant assemblage that included the redwood tree! There have been other changes, too, in the very form of the earth. Alaska and Siberia were once joined by land in what some scientists have referred to as "Amerasia." This world of ours has been a dynamic unit of the universe, has gone through many changes as a planet, and is still changing. (As I write this, our little community is talking about the slight earthquake we felt a few nights ago.)

To understand a little of this, we must realize that our planet is a huge magnet, with two magnetic poles—northward and southward. Those of us who remember our school experiments with iron filings may recall how they arranged themselves in magnetic lines concentrating at the two poles of the magnet.

But the earth's magnetic poles do not coincide with what we know as the north and south poles. These *geographic* poles are formed by the spinning of the earth on its axis. The *magnetic* north pole is on the Boothia Peninsula of Baffin Island, and that is where the compass needle points.

"True north" is in the direction of the spot we call the North Pole. At the North Pole the only direction is south. We look up at the pole star, above the North Pole, and the two stars on the cup of the Great Dipper point to it.

Thinking in cosmic terms, both the magnetic poles and the earth axis poles are variable. We know that day and night are produced by the earth spinning a full turn every twenty-four hours so that any one place alternately faces the sun and faces darkness. Also, the spinning earth slowly tilts toward or away from the sun. Thus we have the seasons. In the far Arctic we have in summer round-the-clock daylight and midnight sun, and in winter, when the earth tilts away from the sun, no sun at all. Yet in some places on the earth, where the Arctic extends far enough south, as in Bering Sea down to the Aleutian Islands, there are a few hours of sunlight even in December.

All these things are well-known facts, of course. But we should understand the variability of all things. Nothing is static, things are changing—our philosophy as well as the earth's forms and phases. Let us look at what happened in our Arctic. Many millions of years ago, we know, there must have been a warm climate, as exemplified by the redwood fossil from St. Lawrence Island. Then recently—as nature measures time—in the Pleistocene, ice covered much of the northern part of the northern hemisphere. What eccentricities in our relation with the life-giving sun could produce such great contrasts?

According to some scientific opinion, a moderate change in the average year-long temperature can bring on an ice age. This can be understood by any of us sojourning in northern latitudes, where the summer is so short that in some places the overflow ice in river valleys thaws away not very long before ice forms again.

At one time in this continent's history, this winter ice did not thaw at all, and year by year ice and snow accumulated until a big part of our earth in the polar region became a great ice sheet of immense thickness. This heavy white mantle extended down over Canada, covering the land that is now fertile farm country. The huge glacier extended southward into what we now know as our northern states—Wisconsin, Michigan, Minnesota—and down the New England coast. And it extended down over what we know as the "taiga" of Eurasia, Scandinavia, and even into the British Isles. What a long winter that was, lasting more than a million years and covering so much of our earth. We cannot help thinking in human terms—what would it have been like to be there then?

Strangely enough, in the later Ice Ages a good part of Alaska and adjacent Siberia was not covered with ice. This was the time when mammoths, mastodons, wild horses, bison, wapiti, giant beavers, and a host of other animals possessed that land. Whenever the universe relents a little and permits a livable spot on one of its planets, the universal energy comes to life and proliferates into the diverse forms which we have learned to know and admire. We find the bones of those creatures today, in Siberia, Interior Alaska, and parts of Canada, and we can picture them inhabiting that favored part of the earth, practically surrounded by vast circumpolar ice.

I remember a day when Dr. Otto William Geist, who collected fossils for the University of Alaska and the American Museum of Natural History, showed me a fossil bison, the skeleton still covered by the hardened, hairless hide. And in Yukon Territory we found mammoth tusks and teeth, bison bones, and lenses of ice in sloughing mud banks—all relating back to Pleistocene life in that country.

But after a great many centuries our relation with the sun changed again—our northern atmosphere became consistently warmer. The ice had to go—but so slowly! However, nature had plenty of time. Everywhere around the globe the glacier's edge moved northward. As the ice retreated, plant and animal life moved in.

Finally, the ice edge moved far enough north that even the Arctic shores of the continents were free of it, and the persistent plant life crowded north as far as there was land. Even the northern seas, with their ever-present living things, were periodically exposed to the air and became more recognizable in our geography.

This was all in the distant past. We have been able to piece together this vital earth history through human curiosity and exciting exploration by scientists who bring to the task a knowledge of facts and natural laws so far comprehended. Once more we have in the Arctic the progress of the seasons as we know them—winter, spring, summer, and fall. Perhaps we do not have the luxuriant plant life of that time millions of years ago suggested by the fossil redwood fragment from St. Lawrence Island, but plants are once more decorating the landscape, and animals have occupied the land and even parts of the polar sea. With the growing awareness of beauty by the human race, the Arctic has much to offer.

But where is the Arctic today—where are its boundaries, in human language? Although the Arctic has once more become able to blossom with lusty life, the icy winter era, millions of years long, left some remnants. All through the world we have glaciers.

Today, more than ever before, we are looking out into space; we are letting our minds go farther out, much farther, than our bodies can go. So let's take our minds on a tour around the world in the north country, just so we can have some idea of what we are talking about here. It will be a hasty look, a far-away look, so as to grasp the outline and the big features of that country up north.

Always there are the seasons to consider. If we were to go on our tour in winter, the whole Arctic would be white; we would not see where the sea ends and the land begins. So let's go on our imaginary journey in summer!

First there is the polar sea, which is mostly white, winter or summer, and somewhere up there, the North Pole—one end of the axis on which the earth is spinning. The central portion of the polar sea is still largely ice-covered, but its surface is restless—there are currents and drifting of its ice, pressures of floes, breaking into ridges. It is a live ocean. Portions of our northern continental shores have some open water for navigation in the proper seasons. This open water freezes over in winter, as does a good portion of Bering Sea and all of Hudson and James Bays. Iceland, despite its chilly name, always has navigable water around it.

We still have glaciers. Most of Greenland is glaciated—our largest remaining continental glacier—and it furnishes many of the icebergs of the North Atlantic. We have glaciers in mountain masses extending far southward on our continents. There are small glaciers in our mountain ranges, particularly in the western part of America. Mount McKinley is perpetually white with ice and snow, and there are other glaciers in the Alaskan mountains, culminating in the picturesque glacier-covered mountains of the southern coast. Far southward, in the Rocky Mountain system, there are mountain glaciers; and on the Eurasian continent we also have them, especially in the high Himalayas.

Suppose we are standing on Greenland and looking west and north. There is the Arctic archipelago, including Baffin Island and many others. They are sparsely occupied with animal life, but on Ellesmere Island we find the small Peary caribou and certain birds, including the blue and snow geese which nest there. Looking toward the south, we see the high, wooded plateau of interior Labrador, dotted with many lakes and streams. Then westward of Hudson Bay is a wide expanse of open tundra which Seton referred to as the "Arctic Prairies." In the western part of Canada, we come to rugged mountains, the northern extension of the Rocky Mountain system. And in Alaska we have several mountain ranges, with a narrow tundra slope extending north to the Arctic Ocean. On the Bering Sea coastline we have an interesting situation—a treeless coastal plain extending down to the Alaska peninsula and the Aleutian Islands chain. There are comparable areas on the Siberian side. It is interesting to note that several Arctic animals live that far south. Finally, across Siberia all the way to Scandinavia there is a coastal strip of Arctic-type land.

On man-made maps we see the Arctic Circle; but in allocating climates around the world, nature knew nothing of the Arctic Circle. The boundary of what we know as the Arctic is extremely variable; in Interior Alaska the boundary is far north of the Arctic Circle, and in Hudson Bay and Bering Sea, far south of it.

Mountaineers measure their exploits by the altitude they have attained, measured in feet. Similarly, Arctic explorers measured their success by the latitude they could reach. From the standpoint of living conditions, if we take the altitude of a southern high mountain, measured in feet, lay it horizontal pointing north and measure it in miles, we would approximate the effect of latitude. Timberline in the southern mountains is comparable with edge of the forest in the north. "Upness" is comparable with "northness."

There are a number of considerations which bear this out. As one example in the plant world, *Dryas octopetala*, the circumpolar mountain avens, is very common in Alaska. There, especially on suitable slopes near timberline, it becomes abundant. It is also found in the high country of the Alaska Range and in the mountains of Norway. Interestingly enough, I found this same plant blooming in the mountains of western Wyoming, but above timberline.

Then I found that this is nothing new. In George Sarton's *Six Wings: Men of Science in the Renaissance*, the author refers to a book by Lobelius, called *Herbals*, published in 1570–71. According to Sarton, Lobelius "remarks on the existence of plants in higher latitudes that could also be observed on high mountains further south. He was apparently the first to make this observation, which was generalized later by the Pyrenean botanist Louis Ramond, and finally introduced into botanical geography by Alexander von Humboldt."

I quote this to show that for centuries we may be unaware of significant observations made by certain intelligent men and have to discover the facts all over again.

Let me mention also certain birds that have the same tendency. The horned lark and the pipit commonly nest on open flatlands in the Arctic. They also nest on flat mesas above timberline in southern mountains. The rosy finch nests in mountain cliffs at and above timberline, in western Wyoming at an elevation of about 11,000 feet. In Alaska, in the Aleutian Islands, it nests at sea level, but the land is treeless, and the bird finds there the same kind of environment as on more southerly peaks. I am not concerned here with the various subspecies—the species is the important thing in this case. Then there are the ptarmigan, which we think of as northern birds. But one of them, the white-tailed ptarmigan, is found as far south as Colorado—always high in the mountains. It occurs also in Glacier Park and the Alaska Range at a much lower elevation, but in the same kind of treeless environment.

Many years ago the biologist Dr. C. Hart Merriam devised a system of life zones. Among them he called the northern one beyond timber the "Arctic Zone" and the one above timberline in the mountains the "Arctic-Alpine Zone." Thus he recognized the similarity between the Far North and the high alpine life associations. He also realized that the timbered area near these zones was different from the timbered area lower down or farther south, and he called them the "Hudsonian" and "Canadian" zones. What I found along the east coast of Hudson Bay and in interior Labrador must have been mostly the Hudsonian.

Speaking of timberline, I recall an experience in the Chisos Mountains of Texas. The plains were all desert, with many charming kinds of cactus and other desert plants. One day I climbed far up in the Chisos Mountains and there came to a lower timberline—the beginning of aspen and other trees I had seen in the northern states.

Life in its various forms adjusts to what it finds in different parts of the planet. And we human beings find it difficult to classify nature's processes into a formula. There is much overlapping, each kind of life finding its niche, forming a "biota" of a kind. But I think we can do best by making the forest edge the southern boundary of the Arctic. Let us in that respect ignore the Arctic Circle. In the Hudson Bay region and interior Labrador the timber goes up nearly to Hudson Strait. In Interior Alaska the timber goes nearly to the Arctic Ocean, but in the Bering Sea region there is an Arctic coastal plain all the way down to the Alaska peninsula and the Aleutians. So the boundary of the Arctic is very irregular around the globe.

Temperature is not the best criterion either. The temperature is much lower south of timberline in Interior Alaska than it is on the Arctic coast. I don't know what the criterion might be. But with all of these unanswered questions, we can still try to enjoy and understand the Arctic.

South for the Winter

M any people who live in snowy places like to go to a warmer place for part of the winter. Nature had established such a procedure many millennia ago, before modem man came on the scene, but for a different reason.

The fact of bird migration is common knowledge. In North America migration has become such an important factor in conservation of our migratory species that we have international treaties to help us coordinate our efforts. But why do so many species of birds leave the northland and spend winters in the south? To help understand that question we must notice what *kinds* of birds have this habit. And it is interesting to follow some of these birds on their journeys.

The birds nesting in northern Scandinavia, Finland, Russia, and the Arctic islands seek parts of southern Europe and Africa to spend the winter. Bengt Berg, the Swedish nature writer, has written a charming book about them, *To Africa with the Migratory Birds*.

One famous migratory flyer is the arctic tern. It is said to nest as far north as there is suitable nesting land, and to winter as far south as there is land. Of course we do not know the travels of any individual bird, and there is a wide variation in "northness" and "southness," but the two geographic extremes would represent an annual wing-powered round-trip of about 22,000 miles!

There are many other long-distance travelers. The golden plover takes off from the southeastern United States for its destination in South America, and it has been stated that these birds cross 6,000 miles of ocean in a single flight!

Another shorebird, the wandering tattler, was for a long time an enigma. We knew that tattlers must nest somewhere in Alaska, but we didn't know where. Then in 1923 my brother and I found a nest on a gravel bar in Mount McKinley National Park. Since then we have found them nesting in various parts of Arctic Alaska. Then again, in December of 1948, I had the privilege of seeing a bit of the other side of the story. A group of us were walking along a beach in northern New Zealand to see what birds we could find. There we found a wandering tattler! That bird had gone to the southern hemisphere to enjoy another summer while there was winter in the Arctic.

The June 1957 issue of the *Sports Fishing Institute Bulletin* gives the following:

WATERFOWL MYSTERY SOLVED

SYLVA, delightful publication of the Ontario Department of Lands and Forests, frequently reports on the disconcerting uncomplicated thinking processes of schoolboys. Its latest gem seems to solve one of the more intriguing scientific mysteries that has long baffled waterfowl experts.

"An excerpt from a teacher's report revealed that this examination question: 'In the fall, why do wild geese fly south?'—stimulated this very logical answer: 'Because it is too far to walk.' "

Life would be much easier on all of us if we could all think clearly as the schoolboys!

Well, let us try to think clearly on this question. We must try to understand life in the Far North. We all know about the migration of birds to warmer countries in the winter, and back north again for the summer. But why do they do that? Why don't they stay south all the time?

I was once asked to take part in a discussion at the Aeromedical Laboratory at the air force base in Fairbanks, Alaska. The subject was laboratory work versus field work in wildlife studies. I don't like that word versus—the idea of "either-or." We need both, but I felt that we often overlook thoughtful field observations because they are too simple and too obvious to be "scientific."

We know that the world is full of life—there are no empty places. Many birds remain year-round in warm climates. But in the Far North food is plentiful in summer, though not available in winter. Then, too, we must keep in mind that some living things have the exploratory impulse—that is why the whole globe is populated.

For instance, there are in the north, swallows that live on insects; sparrows that live on insects and seeds; shorebirds and waterfowl that feed in open water, and many others, all of whom find their chosen food plentiful in summer but not in winter. So they must go south. On the other hand, there are birds, such as the chickadees and woodpeckers, that can find larvae and little morsels in the bark of trees and stay through the winter. The spruce grouse feeds extensively on spruce needles. Although ptarmigan gather in flocks and have local migrations, they and other grouse stay in the north where they have learned to subsist on buds of bushes and some trees. When you travel in the north country during the snow season, these permanent residents are the ones with whom you will share the winter.

There are some interesting sidelights on this behavior—some facts which complicate the results of laboratory experiments in which all birds of a species are presumed to be alike. We assume that all ducks must go south for the winter, and that is generally true. But I have found some exceptions. Both in Hudson Bay and in Alaska, I found limited stretches of water that did not freeze over. There must have been warm springs underground. Here I found mallards spending at least part of the winter—I would say the midwinter. They did not go south as other mallards did. In Alaska they were living on remains of dead salmon and probably other aquatic food.

On the Koyukuk River in Alaska, a group of herring gulls remained at a fox farm one year into the winter, at a time when I was going through there with dogteam. They had found an abundance of fox food attractive and stayed on long after the freeze-up. When I went by, I learned that some had already died, and I doubt if any of them survived the winter. But they tried, and obviously it was the food that attracted them.

I don't know much about the movements of the dipper, or water ouzel, but this lively little bird sometimes finds places in the Far North where portions of streams keep open all winter. There they find a congenial environment—so much so that they have a sprightly winter song.

There are some other bird movements that are dependent on food. In certain winters the snowy owl comes even south of Canada—presumably in those winters when the lemmings and other small rodents are scarce on their customary winter range. There is another aspect I have noticed. Red-tailed and Swainson's hawks and the ferruginous rough-legged hawks, which nest in Wyoming, go farther south for winter. But the American rough-legged hawk, which nests in the Far North, winters in the area vacated by those other hawks!

But what about the mammals? How do they plan for the Arctic winter? They can't fly, and as the boy said, it is too far to walk. They have a variety of ways in which to meet and overcome this seasonal emergency. A few, such as the fur seals, walrus, and whales, simply swim south to open water.

The seals get their food in the sea and are good aquatic animals, but they must breathe. So those that spend the winter in Arctic waters keep breathing holes open in the ice, where they can crawl out and lie beside the hole to rest. When a seal sees a polar bear or an Eskimo approaching, he can dive into his hole. Of course, both of these hunters can wait at such a hole, too. But somehow, the seal and the polar bear are able to live on the polar ice. The arctic fox also ventures out upon the ice to find scraps left by the bear.

When I was on Hudson Bay, several Indians told me that they would sometimes see a long seal trail in the snow. One told me that he had once seen such a trail away back in the caribou country. Do the seals occasionally get frozen out so they can't get back into the water? And does the distant dark line of forest seem to them to be open water?

How about the animals living on the land? There is at least one kind of field mouse in Alaska, the species *Microtus miurus* which my brother calls the hay mouse, that elaborately stores up dried plants and roots for winter use. And it is well known that the coney harvests hay for winter. I have heard their little bleat deep under the snow when I was passing over a rockslide area with a dogteam. The tree squirrels live very well on cones, mushrooms, and other food they can store, and therefore are confined to the woods. The moose can thrive on willow and other browse twigs, and the caribou can paw down through the snow for low vegetation and eat browse species. The agile wolves, foxes, lynx, martens, and weasels, all being meat eaters, live on any other creatures they can kill, or on carrion they can find.

What about the grizzly and black bears, the ground squirrels and marmot, all being chiefly vegetarian? They can't fly, and it is too far to walk. Well, they have to do something about it—so they just sleep through the winter. They simply hibernate and thus avoid all the problems. They, too, have found a way to live year-round in snow country.

This is only a brief summary of the various types of adaptive behavior of the creatures in the North. But it is obvious, from what we can observe, that food is the major requirement for existence in the northern snow country, and that the various bird and mammal species meet the problem in a variety of ways. The result of it all is a sort of balance, so that all parts of our planet can be occupied by some form of life.

What do you see when you travel in the north country? Explorers Stefansson and Nansen have shown us that even on the polar sea there is life—seals, polar bears, arctic foxes, even some birds in appropriate places. On northern lands there are the arctic hares, lemmings, snowy owls, ravens, and of course the fox—all rugged species which like that kind of life. In the wooded places as well as farther north are the reindeer, or caribou, the wolf, red fox, and wolverine. There are flocks of ptarmigan feeding in the willows, trails of the snowshoe rabbit in the forests, and occasionally a moose. A chickadee comes out on some spruce twigs near the trail and chirps cheerily. At night you may hear the hooting of the great horned owl and the distant howl of the wolf, to which your dogs respond. And up among the cliffs live the white mountain sheep.

This and more you may see and hear in winter, north or south of the Arctic Circle. Yes, there is life and beauty in the snowy winter of the North.

But in spite of the many charms of winter, toward the end we look forward to another season. Then great numbers of birds have the same urge to come back north. I remember a late February day in New Mexico when, high in the air, flocks of sandhill cranes were already moving northward. That made me think of a camp I had many years before on the upper Tanana River of Alaska. It was April, and the caribou were just beginning to come back northward over the high snowy mountains of the Alaska Range. The Indians down at Tanana Crossing were all out after caribou to feed themselves and their dogs. All had suffered desperate hunger in the late winter months. Now the caribou were coming back and those people, who lived off the country, would eat again.

My camp was on the lower snow-covered slope of the mountains, where I could watch the migrating caribou bands coming down over the white country above the forest. One morning I heard a clear loud call in the sky, and then a chorus—the familiar bugle of sandhill cranes: "*K-r-r-r-o-o-u-gh!*"

High in the air a large flock was passing over, with long necks reaching out forward, long legs trailing behind. As they came almost over my camp, the flock circled round and round, gaining a higher elevation, then went off out of sight northward. Soon another flock came, circled in the same place, then went on. Flock after flock came over and circled at the same place before going on. Had each one seen my camp, or was there a rising current of air at that spot?

At any rate, the caribou coming over the mountain range, the cranes bugling their way on high as they came from some far away southland, the melting snow in the valley, the feel of the air—all meant spring again.

A couple of years later, in 1924, I had the opportunity to see the cranes on their nesting grounds, the coastal marshes of Bering Sea. Here they performed their nuptial dances, had their nests, and raised their young. It must have been the climax of their year, the most significant period in the northland.

On that visit to the shore of Bering Sea, I watched the first lanes of open water appear in the sea ice. Even while the ice was still prominent in the seascape, the feel in the air, the disappearance of the snow on the coastal plain, and the increasing expanses of open water signaled spring. All this somehow became known to the wintering birds farther south, and they felt the pull of the North. Small birds and large birds, one kind after another, appeared on the tundra.

I was fascinated by the king eiders. Flock after flock they passed, high over the greenish ice masses floating in Bering Sea. Their necks were stretched out, their eyes on the distant horizon still farther north, their flight, their whole being focused on that distant Arctic goal. Up there on the coastal tundra of the farthest north land, in the land of the northernmost lemmings, arctic foxes, and an occasional polar bear, they would break up the migratory camaraderie of large flocks and settle down in pairs to build their nests and raise their families in the Arctic summer.

Of course, there were other migrants, too. There were flocks of glaucous gulls. Those that did not settle down on the tidal shores of Bering Sea headed into the northland—great flocks of them, appearing in the distance like undulating shifts of snow above the dark water.

As I stood on that shore watching flock after flock of king eiders and gulls high above the ice floes, there came to me strong impressions that I have not yet learned to express in words. Perhaps I was impressed by the ability of natural, easy flight—a gift bestowed on those birds by nature through long millennia of practice to perfection. Or perhaps it was another gift—the inherent impulse to go south in fall and come north again to the Arctic in spring.

We have studied various physiological processes, the effect of light and other factors on the movements and changes in animals. But as I stood there and watched the phenomenon of spring migration, I was more than ever conscious of the small distance we have really come in our striving to understand what takes place in the natural world around us.

The Protection of Color

On a day in late May in northern Alaska, I watched a pair of willow ptarmigan. In front of our camp, Lobo Lake was still covered with ice. The male ptarmigan was still white, except for a rich brown on his neck and head. Even on the grayish ice, this bird was conspicuous, and his actions, bold and vivacious, tended to call attention to himself. I had noticed that on the snow-free tundra I could see such a white bird a mile away. While the still-white male was disporting himself out on the ice, the female was slowly poking along on the brown shore. She had already changed completely from the winter white to the speckled brown of summer. I could see her only because she moved, so well did she harmonize with the varied brown of the land. Later in the season, both sexes would have the brown summer plumage, except for the white wings and the black tails that they have year-round. The female, who has the responsibility of incubating the eggs, must harmonize with the background. The male, often seen crowing loudly on top of a nearby knoll or tree, calls attention to himself to protect his mate on the nest.

As I see the white snowshoe rabbit among the willows in the winter woods or a group of ptarmigan out on a snowy mountain slope or an arctic hare on a big stretch of tundra, I am impressed with the thought that surely their whiteness against that snowy background gives them protection. Are all these color aspects caused by natural selection, survival of the fittest? We cannot ignore these logical scientific concepts.

Yet, as I observe different species in the Arctic, I seem to find certain complexities and exceptions to this rule of coloring. The so-called collared lemming of the genus *Dicrostonyx* turns white in winter, but lemmings of this genus down on the first few islands of the Aleutian chain do not turn white in winter, though that is snow country, too. Another lemming, the brown lemming, of the genus *Lemmus*, does not turn white at all, though it lives in the same kind of country. Why? Is it because this lemming lives mostly under the snow? Also, several kinds of voles and red-backed mice, common all through the north country, north as well as south of the Arctic Circle, never turn white. Several kinds of ptarmigan have white winter plumages, but the ruffed grouse, sharp-tailed grouse, and spruce grouse do not. It may be pointed out that these latter grouse live in the woods where the snow color is broken and do not need this white color protection. There is indeed a difference in habitat, yet the snowshoe hare that dwells in the same woods is white during winter.

The mountain sheep may give us something to think about. The Dall sheep of Alaska are white all year-round. They don't turn brown in summer for protection. In summer you can easily see these sheep far off in the landscape. Eastward in northern Canada, in the mountains of Yukon, lives the "saddle-back" sheep, partly dark. Farther south, in British Columbia and beyond, the sheep are dark the year-round, yet they live in snow country in winter.

The snowy owl of the north is white all year, too, and is very conspicuous in the summer landscape. It nests on hummocks on the ground. One season when I had many nests under observation, I found that these owls had large broods of young—at least six to ten—but there was a high rate of mortality. Nesting on the ground, the young could easily leave the nest. When a rainy spell came, I would find many dead young birds near the nests. Is the mortality of young related to the size of the clutch? And why should this owl, which so far as we know has no predatory enemies, be white? To more easily capture lemmings and mice in winter? How about summer?

The great horned owl of the North gives us something to think about, too. It does not turn pure white in winter. We could reason that it lives in the woods where colors are darker, and it has no enemies to prey on it regularly. Yet some of the owls are whitish, markedly so, and are considered by some taxonomists to be a subspecies. Once near the Yukon River in Alaska, I saw a pale and a dark owl at the same nest, and I saw them also in the James Bay region across the continent. Perhaps this owl is in the first stages of becoming white, over a period of many centuries.

We of course know about the white polar bear. Maybe he is white like the snow and ice so that he can sneak up on the dark seals. Some Eskimos, in crawling toward seals lying on the ice, use a white screen in front of them which they shove forward, to simulate the whiteness of the surroundings. At other times they dispense with the white screen and when the seal raises its head to look about, the crawling Eskimo hunter raises his feet and waves them, like another seal waving his hind flippers. At times the Eskimo sits at the breathing hole waiting for the seal to appear. I have seen hawks waiting in the same way at open burrows of the pocket gopher. It is the same hunting technique.

Most of the grizzly bears are brownish, but I have seen a black one, and there are various shades of light color, some blotched with white. On the Tanana River of Alaska were many that were very light, and I collected one for the National Museum which was pure white. The wolf has the same variations, from black to white, though most of them are gray.

As for the caribou, the woodland caribou at the southern side of the range are darker than the barren ground caribou, and the Peary caribou high in the Arctic are extremely light colored. The summer pelage of the caribou is very dark, but they have it for a relatively short season. Perhaps eventually the caribou of the Far North will all be light colored the year-round, like the Alaska mountain sheep.

While we are speaking of color, we should discuss the phenomenon of *color phase*, which is variation in the same species. Let us consider a bird and a mammal—the parasitic jaeger and the arctic fox. In the Far North, the parasitic jaeger is normally light colored, with an occasional dark one, which we refer to as a dark color phase. But in the Aleutian chain farther south, they are nearly all dark, and a light-colored "normal" one is rare.

Similarly, in the Far North the arctic fox is normally white in winter, the dark or blue one being rare. But in the Pribilof and Aleutian Islands they are practically all blue.

This whole question of color is complex. We undoubtedly have here an example of the "survival of the fittest" and natural selection. But we must also view the whole ecology of animal life and take into account all natural influences. We must give attention to genetic forces, too. And with this viewpoint we must again raise the discredited theory of inheritance of acquired characteristics.

Genetic influence is not a sudden thing that can be proven in the laboratory. We must begin to think as nature does, in terms of thousands and millions of years. Changes and migrations occur gradually, over a long period. Did the wolf, with its varied colors, come down from the North? Is the lemming of the genus *Lemmus*, which does not turn white in winter, a more recent immigrant to the Arctic than its cousin, the *Dicrostonyx*, which has been there longer and does turn white?

We are dealing now with millennia of time. It seems extremely likely that among the influences on the colors and habits of animals are oceanic climates, temperatures, precipitation, and many others. For instance, we know that in certain latitudes on the Pacific Coast, where precipitation is heavy, temperature relatively mild, and vegetation luxuriant, birds and mammals tend to be much darker than elsewhere. This tendency shows itself all the way up to southern Alaska. Is this the reason that the dark phases of the parasitic jaeger and the arctic fox are so predominant on those southern islands? I would again emphasize that the Aleutian area, which has even the dark form of *Dicrostonyx*, has snow in winter.

I can't offer theories to answer all these questions. In fact, I want to warn against thinking that a theory answers everything. We should reexamine theories. I believe in science as a way to learn, to find out—and that is our hope. Let us keep open minds, respect others and their ideas, and try our best to penetrate the vast unknown, scientifically and philosophically. I have used natural selection, turning white in winter, merely as an example of the complexities facing us.

Evolution proceeds by diversity, by exploring new ideas. Let us try to find our way. A sojourn in the north country, to see nature at work on the planet's frontier, may give us something to ponder.

THE MEANING FOR MAN

From Nansen's Diary

Exploring is a fundamental impulse, characteristic of all life. We usually think of exploring as a human activity, involving equipment and an expedition, but animals explore, too. Thousands of years ago, the elk, or wapiti, traveled from Eurasia to the United States, following the urge of individuals to seek new country. The mountain sheep came the same way from Siberia. The primitive American horses went the other way, from northwest America over into Siberia and Europe, or so the fossil record indicates.

Perhaps we should examine this impulse to seek new places. Let us consider the elk as an example. Detailed studies have shown us that the main body of such an animal population is conservative. That is, in migration from summer to winter range, and the reverse, most of the animals will go back to the accustomed ranges. After the first migration with their mothers, the young calves become indoctrinated into this same habit.

However, there are a few adventurous individuals who tend to move into new territory, thus extending the total range of the species. Similarly, most of the elk remain in the high mountain country until heavy snow makes them move down, but a few come down earlier.

So the instinct to go into far places, to learn and achieve, is something we have inherited from our early sources. Life itself, evolution, is exploratory.

Arctic exploration by humans is a chapter in mankind's history that is inspiring and important to study. The finest summary I know of is the two-volume work of Fridtjof Nansen, called *In Northern Mists*. It was translated into English and published in 1911 by the Frederick A. Stokes Company.

Nansen approaches the subject in an intelligent and philosophical manner. In his preface he enumerates the changes in ideas from age to age. He says he obtained "... a curious insight into the working of the human mind in its endeavor to subject to itself the world and the universe." He found that much that had been written was undependable, that authors copied what had been published, and that errors and opinions became embedded in tradition. This is a tendency that we find in all history.

Nansen also says: "The majority of the voyages, and those the most important, on which the first knowledge was based, have left no certain record; the greatest steps have been taken by unknown pioneers, and if a halo has settled upon a name here and there, it is the halo of legend."

I would like to quote here another paragraph which illustrates the insight of this man, himself an explorer:

It is not until we come far down into the full daylight of history that we find men setting out with the conscious purpose of exploring the unknown for its own sake. With those early hunters, it was doubtless new ground and new game that drew them on, but they too were attracted, consciously or unconsciously, by the spirit of adventure and the unknown—so deep in the soul of man does this divine force lie, the mainspring, perhaps, of the greatest of our actions. In every part of the world and in every age it has driven man forward on the path of evolution, and as long as the human ear can hear the breaking of waves over deep seas, as long as the human eye can follow the track of the northern lights over silent snowfields, as long as human thought seeks distant worlds in infinite space, so long will the fascination of the unknown carry the human mind forward and upward.

I make no attempt here to go into a comprehensive survey of the great field of exploration, but it is interesting to examine the activities of a few of those men, especially those who have expressed for us the deep feelings they have experienced.

An outstanding example of the nobility of some people occurred at the South Pole. A contest arose among explorers as to who would first reach the South or North Pole, and this had assumed international significance. Two parties, one led by Roald Amundsen and the other by Robert Scott, were striving by different routes and different means to reach the South Pole. Scott's party, trying unsuccessfully to use ponies instead of dogs, struggled southward day by day until they finally arrived at the point where, according to their calculations, there was no more south. They were at the South Pole.

But there they found a shocking disappointment—the Norwegian flag. Amundsen had reached the pole first. Scott had two unexposed negatives left in his camera. With one he took a picture of his group, with the British flag they put in place. With the other he took a picture of the Norwegian flag, an example of human chivalry at its best. These twin negatives later got back to civilization.

Unfortunately, Scott and his party, weakened by hard traveling and hunger, died in their last camp, where a rescue party later found them. According to Scott's own journal, one of his men walked out of the tent into a blizzard and was never seen again. It was believed he had left intentionally so as not to be a burden on the rest of the party. The rescue party who finally reached the camp found there the camera with the exposed negatives and Scott's journal. The last entry was a message to the British people, dated March 25, 1912: "I do not regret this journey, which has shown that Englishmen can endure hardships, help one another, and meet death with as great fortitude as ever in the past. . . . We have been willing to give our lives for this enterprise, which is for the honor of our country." This should rank with the finest last words of those who face the end.

There have been a great many expeditions in the polar sea, various dashes for the poles, voyages to find the Northwest Passage, and expeditions to learn more about the scientific aspects of the polar region. I would like here to refer to two of them.

Vilhjalmur Stefansson made many trips into the polar sea and along the Arctic islands and shores of Canada and Alaska. He wrote important observations and convictions about life in the Arctic, both animal and human. From his northern experience, he reached some philosophical conclusions. He lived much with the Eskimos, appraising their culture, and was probably the first to demonstrate that it was possible to live on parts of the polar sea depending on seals and polar bears. This caused a great deal of controversy among experts, but he emphasized, and science will bear him out, that northern waters are rich in life, and that even the Arctic floes support life, such as seals, polar bears, arctic foxes, and seagulls. He brought out the fact that between them, the seals and bears inadvertently furnished food for white foxes and gulls. Stefansson also experimented with human diet and published his findings.

But one book that caused a lot of wonder and disbelief was his *The Friendly Arctic*. This book, based on Stefansson's life and observations in the North, gives a picture far from the sterile, savage one that had become traditional. His experiences demonstrate the usual hardships, but also the wonderful adventure possible in far places. He brings out a fact that many of those who lived in the old days knew—that winter was the time of social doings, the time for reading among white men, the time for stories and dances among Eskimos. And winter was the season when one could make long trips with dogteam. As *The Friendly Arctic* emphasizes, there is much beauty and adventure up there.

Fridtjof Nansen was one Arctic explorer who deserves our attention. We can visualize him up there on the polar ice. He was an explorer with physical strength and courage, and at the same time he was a poet, artist, devoted scientist, philosopher, and a most worthy human being. After his exploits in the polar seas, he did humanitarian work and for many years strove to promote the concept of peace in a snarling world.

Nansen's Arctic experience is presented in his two-volume *Farthest North*, published in 1897 and illustrated with his own watercolors. After his crossing of Greenland and his study of other voyages and evidences of polar currents, he became convinced that if he could place a ship in the ice, a current would take it across the North Pole and on into the Atlantic Ocean in the course of several years. He believed that "a current flows at some point between the Pole and Franz Josef Land from the Siberian Arctic Sea to the east coast of Greenland." With a specially built ship, the *Fram*, Nansen left Norway in June 1893 and took out into the Kara Sea in August. From all over the world he had received applications from men who wanted to go with him. We still find that adventurous spirit in the world today, among young people who would like to go, not for money, but to do and see, and have a rich experience. Nansen deeply felt his responsibility, conscious that all of Norway enthusiastically approved and relied on his judgment. He thought to himself: "Ay, truly, it is a responsible task we are undertaking, when the whole nation are with us like this. What if the whole thing should turn out a huge disappointment!"

And he wrote also: "You may shrug your shoulders as much as you like at the beauties of nature, but it is a fine thing for a people to have a fair land, be it never so poor. Never did this seem clearer to me than now when I was leaving it."

In a public address, Nansen referred to the possibility of reaching the North Pole but commented: "I am, however, of the opinion that this is of small import: *it is not to seek for the exact mathematical point that forms the northern extremity of the earth's axis that we set out, for to reach this point is intrinsically of small moment. Our object is to investigate the great unknown region that surrounds the pole*, and these investigations will be equally important from a scientific point of view whether the expedition passes over the polar point itself or at some distance from it."

Nansen found it hard to leave his family, and in writing of his start, he says, "It was the darkest hour of the whole journey."

After they sailed through the Kara Sea and into the ice, it took a long time to slowly drift with the ice across the Arctic Ocean—many months, winter and summer, of making observations on the currents, making journeys out over the ice, reading books aboard ship, and becoming intimate with this lonesome life beyond the limits of all land. Nansen kept a careful diary, noting not only scientific facts, but also his feelings and reactions to what they saw. Nansen's reactions were decidedly varied. Ice was the major factor in their environment. In some excerpts from that diary, we can vicariously live that journey through what was literally the "frozen North." On September 26 he writes:

Beautiful weather. The sun stands much lower now. I wandered about over the floe towards evening. Nothing more wonderfully beautiful can exist than the Arctic night. It is dreamland, painted in the imagination's most delicate tints, it is color etherealised. One shade melts into the other, so that you cannot tell where one ends and the other begins, and yet they are all there. No forms—it is all faint dreamy colour music, a far-away long-drawn-out melody on muted strings. Is not all life's beauty high, and delicate, and pure like this night? Give it brighter colours, and it is no longer so beautiful. The sky is like an enormous cupola, blue at the zenith, shading down into green, and then into lilac and violet at the edges. Over the ice-fields there are cold violet-blue shadows, with lighter pink tints where a ridge here and there catches the last reflection of the vanished day. Up in the blue of the cupola shine the stars, speaking peace as they always do, those unchanging friends. In the south stands a large red-yellow moon, encircled by a yellow ring and light golden clouds floating on the blue background. Presently the aurora borealis shakes over the vault of heaven its veil of glittering silver—changing now to yellow, now to green, now to red. It spreads, it contracts again, in restless change, next it breaks into waving, many-folded bands of shining silver, over which shoot billows of glittering rays; and then the glory vanishes. Presently it shimmers in tongues of flame over the very zenith; and then again it shoots a bright ray right up from the horizon, until the whole melts away in the moonlight, and it is as though one heard the sigh of a departing spirit. Here and there are left a few waving streamers of light, vague as a foreboding—they are the dust from the aurora's glittering cloak. But now it is growing again; new lightnings shoot up; and the endless game begins afresh. And all the time this utter stillness, impressive as the symphony of infinitude. I have never been able to grasp the fact that this earth will some day be spent and desolate and empty. To what end, in that case, all this beauty, with not a creature to rejoice in it? Now I begin to divine it. *This* is the coming earth—here are beauty and death. But to what purpose? Ah, what is the purpose of all these spheres? Read the answer if you can in the starry blue firmament.

On another occasion he describes a glorious display, which brings living memories to those of us who have witnessed such Arctic beauty. After enumerating the details, he writes:

It was an endless phantasmagoria of sparkling colour, surpassing anything that one can dream. Sometimes the spectacle reached such a climax that one's breath was taken away; one felt that now something extraordinary must happen—at the very least the sky must fall. But as one stands in breathless expectation, down the whole thing trips, as if in a few quick, light scale-runs, into bare nothingness. There is something most undramatic about such a *denouement*, but it is all done with such confident assurance that one cannot take it amiss, one feels one's self in the presence of a master who has the complete command of his instrument. With a single stroke of the bow he descends lightly and elegantly from the height of passion into quiet, everyday strains, only with a few more strokes to work himself up into passion again.

Yes, those are the northern lights, beauty in the polar regions. But as time went on, Nansen thought of home, and he experienced many moods. One time in the Fiordlands of New Zealand, I was caught on the face of a steep bluff when darkness came on. I didn't dare to climb down in the pitch dark, and I didn't dare to lie down and sleep for fear of rolling off the ledge. So, aside from a few short periods of dozing sitting with head on knees, I stood through the night. It seemed an eternity. As Nansen and his men spent summers and winters drifting with the ice, it must have seemed an eternity, too. But they had a good library on the ship, and they had social doings, including a ship's newspaper.

I have quoted Nansen's appreciation of the delicate beauties of the Arctic night. But on Christmas Day, when no doubt he was lonesome and his thoughts were far away over the ice at his home, he wrote:

> But, O, Arctic night, thou art like a woman, a marvelously lovely woman. Thine are the noble, pure outlines of antique beauty, with its marble coldness. On thy smooth brow, clear with the clearness of ether, is no trace of compassion for the little sufferings of despised humanity, on thy pale beautiful cheek no blush of feeling. Among thy raven locks, waving out into space, the hoar-frost has sprinkled its glittering crystals. The proud lines of thy throat, thy shoulders' curves, are so noble, but, oh! unbendingly cold; thy bosom's white chastity is feelingless as the snowy ice. Chaste, beautiful, and proud, thou floatest through ether over the frozen sea, thy glittering garment, woven of aurora beams, covering the vault of heaven. But sometimes I divine a twitch of pain on thy lips, and endless sadness dreams in thy dark eye.
>
> Oh, how tired I am of thy cold beauty! I long to return to life. Let me get home again, as conqueror or as beggar; what does that matter? But let me get home to begin life anew. The years are passing here, and what do they bring? Nothing but dust, dry dust, which the first wind blows away; new dust comes in its place, and the next wind takes that too. Truth? Why should we always make so much of truth? Life is more than cold truth, and we live but once.

Somewhat later, in February, we find him writing in the same vein:

Yes, it is all very well—we snowshoe, sledge, read both for instruction and amusement, write, take observations, play cards, chat, smoke, play chess, eat and drink; but all the same it is an execrable life in the long run, this—at least so it seems to me at times. When I look at the picture of our beautiful home in the evening light, with my wife standing in the garden, I feel as if it were impossible that this could go on much longer. But only the merciless fates know when we shall stand there together again, feeling all life's sweetness as we look out over the smiling fjord. . . . Taking everything into calculation, if I am to be perfectly honest, I think this is a wretched state of matters.

He makes some calculations, then pessimistically says: "At best, if things go on as they are doing now, we shall be home in eight years."

Again:

Oh! at times this inactivity crushes one's very soul; one's life seems as dark as the winter night outside; there is sunlight upon no part of it except the past and the far, far distant future. I feel as if I *must* break through this deadness, this inertia, and find some outlet for my energies. Can't something happen? Could not a hurricane come and tear up this ice, and set it rolling in high waves like the open sea? Welcome danger, if it only brings us the chance of fighting for our lives—only lets us move onwards! The miserable thing is to be inactive onlookers, not to be able to lift a hand to help ourselves forwards. It wants ten times more strength of mind to sit still and trust in your theories and let nature work them out without your being able so much as to lay one stick across another to help, than it does to trust in working them out by your own energy—that is nothing when you have a pair of strong arms.

Then he becomes aware of his sad attitude and writes:

Here I sit, whining like an old woman. Did I not know all this before I started? Things have not gone worse than I expected, but on the contrary, rather better. Where is now the serene hopefulness that spread itself in the daylight and the sun? Where are those proud imaginings now that mounted like young eagles towards the brightness of the future? Like broken-winged, wet crows they leave the sunlit sea, and hide themselves in the misty marshes of despondency. Perhaps it will all come back again with the south wind; but no—I must go and rummage up one of the old philosophers again.

And so we drift along with this virile man who was also a sensitive poet and philosopher. I think of my one night on the cliff in New Zealand, when I undertook to count the seconds in each hour to make the time pass, but that was only one night. This group of men were drifting in the polar sea day after day and month after month, and they were homesick.

In the spring they were still watching the northward drift eagerly, that their theories might prove well-founded. In Nansen's diary of the next June 15 he writes:

This is the first ice-bound expedition that has not spent the summer spying after open water, and sighing and longing for the ice to disperse. I only wish it may keep together, and hurry up and drift northwards. Everything in this life depends on what one has made up one's mind to. One person sets forth to sail in open water, perhaps to the very Pole, but gets stuck in the ice and laments; another is prepared to get stuck in the ice, but will not grumble even should he find open water. It is the safer plan to expect the least of life, for then one often gets the most.

Nansen also expressed his thoughts on perpetual daylight. In many places, where we have enjoyed a variety of activity, perpetual daylight has rather been an attraction, though in camp it may interfere with sleeping. But as they drifted there on the polar sea day after day, I suppose anything perpetual must become monotonous. To put sunlight into a painting there must be shadows. Certainly circumstances affect our feelings about anything.

In June of that first year, we find in Nansen's diary:

> Now I am almost longing for the polar night, for the everlasting wonderland of the stars with the spectral northern lights, and the moon sailing through the profound silence. It is like a dream, like a glimpse into the realms of fantasy. There are no forms, no cumbrous reality—only a vision woven of silver and violet ether, rising up from earth and floating out into infinity. . . . But this eternal day, with its oppressive actuality, interests me no longer—does not entice me out of my lair.

And then, in trying to understand, he writes: "Ah! Life's peace is said to be found by holy men in the desert. Here, indeed, there is desert enough; but peace—of that I know nothing. I suppose it is holiness that is lacking."

But it was not all monotony and homesickness for these men so subjected to the trial of patience. They made their daily observations in the interest of science, recorded longitude, latitude, open lanes of water appearing. Occasionally they found a polar bear, and where there were polar bears at sea, there had to be seals or similar food. And in the summer sun new forms of life appeared. On July 30 we read that they had been drifting southward, and Nansen writes:

> But it occupies my thoughts no longer. I know well enough there will be a change some time or other, and the way to the stars leads through adversity. I have found a new world; and that is the world of animal and plant life that exists in almost every freshwater pool on the ice-floe. From morning till evening and till late in the night I am absorbed with the microscope and see nothing around me; I live with these tiny beings in their separate universe, where they are born and die, generation after generation, where

they pursue each other in the struggle for life, and carry on their love affairs with the same feelings, the same sufferings, and the same joys that permeate every living being, from these microscopic animalcules up to man—self-preservation and propagation, that is the whole story. Fiercely as we human beings struggle to push our way through the labyrinth of life, their struggles are assuredly no less fierce than ours—one incessant, restless hurrying to and fro, pushing all others aside, to burrow out for themselves what is needful to them.

He makes a significant biological report when he says: "And these are small, one-celled lumps of viscous matter, teeming in thousands and millions on nearly every single floe over the whole of this boundless sea, which we are apt to regard as the realm of death. Mother Nature has a remarkable power of producing life everywhere—even this ice is a fruitful soil for her."

These microscopic forms of life, diatoms and algae, were abundant in the pools of melted snow, forming dark spots on the ice surface. He found infusoria and flagellates, and even some bacteria.

In a struggle of patience there are ups and downs. And so in that long drift in the polar ice, there is an entry in October that is more cheerful:

> Oct. 4. Personally I must say that things are going well with me; much better than I could have expected. Time is a good teacher; that devouring longing does not gnaw as hard as it did. Is it apathy beginning? Shall I feel nothing at all by the time ten years have passed? Oh! sometimes it comes on with all its old strength—as if it would tear me in pieces! But this is a splendid school of patience. Much good it does to sit wondering whether they are alive or dead at home; it only almost drives one mad.

Nansen was inspired again when he wrote on Oct. 15:

We are moving northwards, and meanwhile the Arctic night is making its slow and majestic entrance. The sun was low today; I did not see it because of banks of clouds in the south, but it still sent its light up over the pale sky. There the full moon is now reigning, bathing the great ice plain and the drifting snow in its bright light. How a night such as this raises one's thoughts! It does not matter if one has seen the like a thousand times before; it makes the same solemn impression when it comes again; one cannot free one's mind from its power. It is like entering a still, holy temple, where the spirit of nature hovers through the place on glittering silver beams, and the soul must fall down and adore— adore the infinity of the universe.

Here again he had yielded himself to the beauty and charm inherent in the Arctic.

We find a delightful vein in this sensitive soul's journal of November 11:

But the northern lights, with their eternally shifting loveliness, flame over the heavens each day and each night. Look at them; drink oblivion and drink hope from them; they are even as the aspiring soul of man. Restless as it, they will wreathe the whole vault of heaven with their glittering, fleeting light, surpassing all else in their wild loveliness, fairer than even the blush of dawn; but, whirling idly through empty space, they bear no message of a coming day. The sailor steers his course by a star. Could you but concentrate yourselves, too, oh northern lights, you might lend your aid to guide the wildered wanderer. But dance on, and let me enjoy you; stretch a bridge across the gulf between the present and the time to come, and let me dream far, far ahead into the future.

Oh, thou mysterious radiance, what art thou, and whence comest thou? Yet why ask? Is it not enough to admire thy beauty and pause there? Can we at best get beyond the outward show of things? What would it profit even if we could say that it is an electric discharge or currents of electricity through the upper regions of the air, and were we able to describe in minutest detail how it all came to be? It would be mere words. We know no more what an electric current really is, than what the aurora borealis is. . . . Happy is the child. . . . We, with all our views and theories, are not in the last analysis a hair's breadth nearer the truth than it.

Here is the poet and scientist, struggling to appraise a natural phenomenon, and this entry, when studied carefully with a broad mind, has in it some profound truth.

Two days later Nansen has a delightful frolic over the ice, brimful of the exuberance that wells up uncontrollably at times:

A delightful snowshoe run in the light of the full moon. Is life a vale of tears? Is it such a deplorable fate to dash off like the wind, with all the dogs skipping around one, over the boundless expanse of ice through a night like this in the fresh crackling frost, while the snowshoes glide over the smooth surface, so that you scarcely know you are touching the earth, the stars hang high in the blue vault above? This is more, indeed, than one has any right to expect of life; it is a fairy tale from another world, from a life to come.

He speaks here of snowshoes, but we know them now as skis. Often those men made sallies over the ice on skis, with the dogs. He speaks of it again, the next day:

How marvelous are these snowshoe runs through this silent nature! The ice-fields stretch all around bathed in the silver moonlight; here and there dark, cold shadows project from the hummocks, whose sides faintly reflect the twilight. Far, far out a dark line marks the horizon, formed by the packed-up ice, over it a shimmer of silvery vapour and above all the boundless deep blue, starry sky, where the full moon sails through the ether. But in the south is a faint glimmer of day, low down a dark, glowing red hue, and higher up a clear yellow and pale green arch, that loses itself in the blue above. The whole melts into a pure harmony, one and indescribable. At times one longs to be able to translate such scenes into music. What mighty chords one would require to interpret them.

Silent, oh, so silent! You can hear the vibrations of your own nerves. I seem as if I were gliding over and over these plains into infinite space. Is not this an image of what is to come? Eternity and peace are here. Nirvana must be cold and bright as such an eternal star night. What are all our research and understanding in the midst of this infinity?

So through the Arctic winters and summers, the *Fram* drifted with the ice across the polar sea. All were comfortable aboard. They went out on skis, shot occasional polar bears for food, and made their daily observations. The ups and downs of the spirit are recorded in Nansen's diary.

But then Nansen and his men shaped another plan. Two of them would travel on land with dogs, sleds, and kayaks while the ship would be left under the command of Otto Sverdrup to continue its drift with the ice. Nansen and Frederik Johansen went off on their journey on March 14, 1895. In a way this must have been a relief to those two, starting off across the ice with sleds. There was danger, of course, but above all there was something to do—these were explorers, people who crave to do. They had a long and eventful journey, wintering on the west coast of Franz Josef Land, but eventually made their way back to Norway at the same time as the *Fram*—more than three years after their departure. What a homecoming for them, for Norway, and for the world!

This is not the place to enumerate all the adventures of both parties. But it is important for us now, years later, to evaluate such men, to see if what they did has significance for us. Mankind is still exploring. We are striving to find our way into the future. I have quoted a great deal from Nansen's journal to help us think this out. There were explorers long before recorded history. Men have gone forth in far places, for glory, prestige, adventure. Any or several of these motivations have moved men to face dangers and death. They were often finding new lands, discovering new territory for the prestige of a nation, opening new trade routes, or gathering scientific information.

Have we now begun new exploration, seeking new avenues for the future? As Nansen so often stated, we do not yet know where we are going, but it is important that we choose the right direction. To keep ourselves physically strong, to seek to know more and understand more through our scientific techniques, and to appreciate the beauties of the universe—these seem to be safe guideposts for us.

I should like to offer one more quotation from this very sensitive Arctic explorer, an entry in the diary that foreshadows Nansen's humanitarian activities in later years. In the chapter entitled "The Winter Night," we learn about the rough ice, the monotony of that feature of the seascape, and how, at one point, Nansen longed for snow to soften things:

> Why will it not snow? Christmas is near, and what is Christmas without snow, thickly falling snow? We have not had one snowfall all the time we have been drifting. The hard grains that come down now and then are nothing. Oh, the beautiful white snow, falling so gently and silently, softening every hard outline with its sheltering purity. There is nothing more deliciously restful, soft and white. This snowless plain is like a life without love—nothing to soften it. The marks of all the battles and pressures of the ice stand forth just as when they were made, rugged and difficult to move among. Love is life's snow. It falls deepest and softest into the gashes left by the fight—whiter and purer than snow itself. What is life without love? It is like this ice, a cold, bare, rugged mass, the wind driving it and rending it and forcing it together again, nothing to cover over the open rifts, nothing to break the violence of the collisions, nothing, nothing but bare, rugged drift ice.

Music of the Spheres

So many of our experiences in the Arctic have to do with snow and ice and low temperature that the impression arises that the north country is a frozen wasteland. Also, some who have undertaken to write about the North think that the habits of some people on the northern frontier is all there is to the North. One man who wrote a book on Alaska was so obsessed with the drinking and gambling in the communities he visited—the sordid side of human character, which you can find anywhere in the world—that he felt those things represented Alaska, and said it was "a hell of a place."

Another book, a novel of Alaska, had as a subtitle: "Women and gold and a raw new country—the brawling, lusty, turbulent story of a man who challenged the untamed frontier." And the author, using strong language, says in part: "Some Alaskans reading this will become angry. . . . That is a matter of opinion and I am willing to argue my point, any time, anywhere, so long as there is a bottle of whiskey to stimulate the conversation."

Well, that is the frontier anywhere in the world, as some people see it. It all depends on a person's viewpoint whether a place is a hell or a heaven. But a proper appraisal of any area, be it tropics, desert, or Far North, depends on human attitude and understanding.

Ice, snow, cold—the Arctic wastelands. A barren inhospitable part of the earth, we think—a traditional view nurtured over the years at comfortable southern firesides. Is it? Is it, then, such a fierce, man-destroying, savage part of our globe, a land which destroys or maims the sensitivity of those who venture above the Arctic Circle? There is no question about it, ice and snow and cold can be an obstacle, a serious discomfort. Those of us who have spent some years in snow country can tell of many mishaps, struggles, worries. But at this point I am reminded of what Georg Brochmann says in his book *Humanity and Happiness*, part of which was written in Norway during the Occupation. He said in substance that the greatest happiness comes when one overcomes an obstacle.

How then shall we evaluate ice and snow? There are times when almost anything can be an obstacle to what we are doing at the moment.

Shall we not welcome obstacles that give us strength? Why do men and women climb mountains on their own two feet? Why do some people ignore the outboard motor and prefer the hand-wielded paddle to any other form of water transportation? Why do people seek those high-latitude areas of our world when they could remain at a southern home in comfort? For that matter, why do athletes compete for personal achievement?

I believe it was Oliver Allston who told of talking with an explorer and asking him why he made his difficult journeys. The explorer replied, in effect, "It's fun. Just fun. Explorers give you all kinds of reasons for their trips, scientific and otherwise. But really they like to do it. It's fun."

In the Far North, we do sometimes meet hardships. But somehow these have a way of fading in importance while other aspects of the North remain vividly alive and enrich us.

In September 1917, after our party had crossed Labrador, we left Fort Chimo on the supply ship *Nascaupie*. We were passing the coast of Baffin Island, whose rocky shores were already flecked with snow. Winter was setting in, and from my position on the deck of the little ship, those shores looked bleak and forbidding. I shivered at the prospect. Here I was looking out at weather from a comfortable perch, as we often look out at winter from a warm home.

Among the few passengers was a Hudson's Bay Company trader who had spent several winters on that shore of Baffin Island. One day he was telling us some of his experiences. He was a slightly built man, but a vital, dynamic person. As he told of his impressions of the sea ice on certain days, he groped for words, but there was a poetic ardor in his voice as he tried to describe and help us visualize the colors he had seen.

"The blue! The green! It's—it's hardly believable. The colors at the broken edges of the jumbled ice!" He gesticulated to emphasize his enthusiasm. "The shades of green!" he repeated.

Here was a man who had lived for a time where people were scarce, in the "arctic wasteland," and he could tell us vividly of the beauty he had found in ice. The snowy bluffs of Baffin Island past which we were steaming took on a new aspect for me. I recalled the time in the spring of 1915, on

Hudson Bay, when Wetunnok and I went out on the ice and came on a lane of open water, as I mentioned in an earlier chapter. Now I recalled again the greens on the edge of the ice and the dark blue of the water, in contrast to the white of the seagulls and the colors on the eiders.

Again in the spring of 1924 I saw the floating ice floes with blue and green shades, and again the dark blue water, and above it all great flocks of seagulls and of king eiders on their way farther north to nest. Another beautiful memory picture.

On the other side of our planet, one of the antarctic expeditions of the fifties had as a member an artist, Leland Curtis, who put onto canvas his impressions and interpretations of the antarctic snow and ice. Later Leland showed me some reproductions of these paintings. It would be futile to try to put into words what this artist put on his canvas. He had a feeling for the lights and shades, the delicate colors, of the antarctic icescapes. Here again is a man who comprehends the beauty in our world, wherever he may be.

This appreciation of beauty began long ago, really before man appeared on the earth. We are beginning to understand now that many of our fellow creatures, some birds, mammals, and even those lower in the scale of evolution, had the rudiments of appreciation of sound. And this has come down to us in a more explicit form. Several centuries ago Pythagoras began experimenting with musical principles, particularly musical intervals as he found them on his harp. And his followers, the so-called Pythagoreans, had the feeling that there must be some kind of harmony of sound among the millions of stars they could see in the heavens. They referred to it as "the music of the spheres."

True enough, modern research has revealed no music as such out there, though recently certain radar records have been received from outer space. But in spite of those early material misconceptions, many of us feel today that our appreciation of beauty, our imagination, and our curiosity, resulting in science—all are attributes which we have inherited and developed through the many ages. We would do well, for a richer and more meaningful life, to develop and respect each of our abilities of that kind. Perhaps we should give thought to our ancestors and feel humbly grateful for the beginnings of thoughtful regard and enjoyment of our land. We should think about what we have learned about those relatives of ours, how they became aware of their surroundings, developed an artistic sense, and expressed their impulse in many artistic manifestations—music, painting, dancing, and poetry. They looked out upon the universe with wonder and respect, and began satisfying their curiosity by what we now know as science. Their intelligence, imagination, and interest in life led them to lay the foundations of religion and philosophy. All this was in response to an inner urge that we still have and still do not fully understand.

A few days ago we were listening to a phonograph record from *The Song of Norway*, the operetta based on the music of Grieg. In one of the songs is a mention of "the music of the spheres." Our minds still go off into the universe!

I was lying on the ground, resting near a pond where there were many ducks and two trumpeter swans. It was October. I looked up into a willow, its long yellow leaves dancing in the wind. And beyond them I saw the clouds against the blue sky. My thoughts too went up there into the universe. I couldn't help it. After all, we are often inspired by the wind in the tops of pine trees. As I lay there, I thought of the fine book *Wind in the Willows*. Our thoughts do sometimes reach for the heights.

A neighbor told me a little incident. His two-year-old boy, just old enough to be aware of things, toddled out on the porch one evening and suddenly, for the first time, saw the stars in the sky. He pointed up excitedly and in his childish voice exclaimed: "Those lights!"

The awakening of the child, his emergence into the natural world— are we able to remember when we had such childlike adventure?

The development of a child may, in a way, suggest the development of a race. The long human procession has also had its awakening and spiritual growth. We were peeking at the stars and studying and speculating about them even before we invented the telescope. More recently we have seen on Mars a white area, like ice, which appears at certain seasons and at other times disappears. Does Mars have seasons like ours? And an Arctic?

The passenger steamer *Yukon* passed Cape Hinchinbrook, leaving

Prince William Sound, and started across the Gulf of Alaska. As night was settling down the air was still, the water smooth. Off across the water rose the Fairweather Range, the mountains shining out a snowy white silhouette against the dark sky, and above them were the clear stars and a bright moon. It was the kind of scene that would be the highlight of any voyage, especially along the southern Alaskan coast—the beauty, the serenity, and the comfortable companionship that grows among the passengers in the presence of beauty that is shared by all.

Then something began to happen. In the northern sky, above the shining mountains, a few long shafts of white light arose. More appeared, broad sheaths of white, literally "out of thin air." Then the star-studded sky came alive. The light shafts shimmered, joined together, made long bands, large masses—surely something alive up there! By this time passengers were all crowded out on the upper deck, as though they wanted to get as close to the sky as possible.

Then came the colors. Rainbowlike "curtains" formed. A band of the purest green ran along the edge of the arc, and about the same time we became aware of a band of lavender that glowed into being, parallel to the green. It reminded one of a rainbow display, but here was a continual changing, a movement of shapes and colors. It covered much of the northern sky.

Among the eagerly gazing passengers gathered there was an old-time Alaskan. To impress these *chechakos*, he airily spoke of "seeing these lights often up on the Koyukuk, playing right down in the grass roots!" Of course, those who live in the North are very familiar with this phenomenon. Mardy and I had also seen it often, but we concluded that this display on the southern coast of Alaska was the best we had ever seen.

The old-time Alaskan who had seen the northern lights "down in the grass roots" suggested a slightly different opinion. Many people in the North declare that at times they could *hear* the northern lights. Some scientists do not wish to deny this, although they themselves have not heard them. Neither have I consciously heard them; but Mardy declares positively that at times during the years when she was growing up in Alaska, she heard the northern lights make a sound. Apparently we don't know—we have much to learn. As we watched that display from the deck of our ship, I thought of what science says about the aurora. It is caused primarily by minute particles from the sun coming in contact with the magnetic field of the earth. Again, it will take us some time to understand all about it.

On that September night in 1926, one of our fellow passengers was the late William Finley, naturalist and nature writer. The three of us stood together watching the bands of light—broad horizontal sheets, vertical shafts—until the whole northern sky was filled clear up to the zenith and beyond.

Finally, conscious of his writing profession, he exclaimed, "How could a fellow describe a thing like this!"

We watched silently for a while. Then he proposed: "Suppose, tonight, each one of us try, when we go to our cabins; suppose each of us three, independently, write his own version of what we are watching here."

Later, in the cabin, I did consider writing down my impressions, but I didn't know how to begin. I never knew whether Finley tried. Perhaps we all felt this was an experience beyond the skill of pen. As Van Dyke said, "The best part of a trip is the part that escapes the notebook."

And I wonder why I am trying to tell about it now. Perhaps it is just the universal impulse to try to share experience.

The aurora borealis well represents natural attributes that can enrich human living. Then think of the whole northern winter. If you are far enough south in the Arctic zone, the sun rises on a short arc in the south, sunrise merging into sunset. But eventually comes the midnight sun of summer, when the ice melts, flowers bloom, many more birds arrive, and there are the caribou, wolves, and grizzlies, all finding the North a good place.

We have been blessed with the power to appreciate beauty—in color, form, and sound; we have been endowed with curiosity, the urge to reason things out scientifically, to wonder about ourselves and the universe. And we have imagination. Could there be a finer assemblage of powers conferred on any living creature? Poetry, Art, Science, Wonder, Awe, Philosophy—and enthusiasm. What a heritage we have, if we only let it operate! And *all* of these are by no means incompatible.

Along with scientific search for truth, which must be paramount in all human endeavor, there is emerging an awareness of the poetic implications in what we learn. Science and aesthetics seem to be contradictory as they are sometimes presented to us. The "music of the spheres" may not accord with the scientific facts we have learned so far, but that concept illustrates nevertheless a wholesome human impulse—to seek beauty. When we attain a new understanding of something in the field of science, the thoughtful scientist is filled with wonder and a degree of reverence for what we only partially understand. A poetic appreciation of life, combined with a knowledge of nature, creates humility, which in turn becomes the greatness in man.

Sun and moon and stars, the northern lights, the rising and the setting, day and night, summer and winter—the pageant of the North. All this and its precious wild creatures, I have known.

And I now also know how greatly privileged I have been.

Herring gull soars over Last Lake in the Brooks Range.

Caribou are the one resource on which many Eskimos based their whole economy.
(Courtesy of the National Park Service)

Spectacled eider drake.

Young Pacific eider at Izembek Bay.

Arctic tern, summering at Hooper Bay after its long flight from the south.

Ptarmigan in winter plumage.

Two views of a snowy owl at its nest

APPENDIX

Biographical Note

Olaus Murie's parents came to Moorhead, Minnesota, from Norway in 1888, the year before he was born. Though his father had been educated as a Norwegian Army officer, this was a period when many thousands were leaving the Old World for the exciting promises of the New. Within ten years, however, Olaus's mother was left a widow, almost penniless and with three young sons to rear. They had a tiny house, one cow, and little else. The whole family had to work hard, but through it all Mrs. Murie never gave up her dream of an education for her children.

Pink winter sunsets forever after reminded Olaus of those cold winter days in Moorhead when he delivered pails of milk before and after school, and dragged firewood home from the forest on his little sled. From the time he was eight years old, he worked at anything he could find to do, chiefly in gardens and on truck farms. At first he was paid with vegetables, then with a few coins, and finally with "man's wages" of a dollar a day.

Olaus always said, however, that no one could have had a better boyhood. In addition to hard work there were always joys—the days when he, his brothers, and their friends roamed the woods along the Red River, gathering wood and fishing for needed food, but also skating in winter, swimming in summer, and camping out in a thickly wooded area which they called "The Wilderness!" A great world opened to Olaus when his fourth-grade teacher read aloud Ernest Thompson Seton's *Two Little Savages*. After that, he devoured all the Seton books he could find. This was the beginning of his great love of nature and wildlife of every kind.

After finishing high school, Olaus entered Fargo College, just across the river from Moorhead. When his biology professor there took a position at Pacific University in Forest Grove, Oregon, he made it possible for Olaus to work his way through the university and obtain his bachelor's degree. For two years following his graduation in 1912, he was employed by the Oregon State Game Commission. Then, from 1914 through 1917, he was field naturalist and curator of mammals for the Carnegie Museum of Pittsburgh. (Two Carnegie expeditions, one into the Hudson Bay country, the other across the Labrador Peninsula, are described in this book.)

Olaus Murie's career as a naturalist was interrupted when he enlisted as a balloon observer in World War I, but it resumed with an appointment in the US Biological Survey (now the Fish and Wildlife Service) in 1920. His first assignment there was a study of the life history and migrations of the caribou of Alaska and Yukon Territory. This project continued for four years, during which he also carried out assignments to study waterfowl in the Hooper Bay region and brown bears on the Alaska Peninsula. One result of these years was the publication of No. 54 of the North American Fauna Series, *Alaska-Yukon Caribou*.

In Alaska Olaus met the young woman who was to share his life and many of his wilderness enterprises as well. He and Mardy were married in August 1924 in a little log mission church at Anvik on the Yukon. For a honeymoon they traveled, first by boat and then by dogteam, into the heart of the Endicott Mountains of the Brooks Range, in further pursuit of information about the caribou. Two years later found them journeying by motorboat and poling boat to the headwaters of the Old Crow River, with their friend Jesse Rust as assistant and their ten-month-old son, Martin, as a special passenger.

After Olaus received his master's degree from the University of Michigan in 1927, the Muries moved to Jackson Hole, Wyoming. There would be assignments and expeditions to many places, but from that time on, Jackson Hole would be their home. The mountains on the east side of Jackson Hole are the summer range of most of the elk in the famous Jackson Hole herd, and Olaus was to make a complete study of their life history. It was quite a party that led the pack horses into those hills—Olaus, Mardy, two-year-old Martin, two-month-old Joanne, and their assistant, fifteen-year-old Billy Sheldon, son of naturalist-sportsman Charles Sheldon, who had urged the government to undertake the elk herd study. Four years later the Muries' third child, Donald, was born.

In 1945 Olaus resigned from the Fish and Wildlife Service to become director of The Wilderness Society, and there followed fifteen active, challenging years in the world of conservation. Under a Fulbright grant, Olaus was also leader of a scientific expedition to the fiordlands of New Zealand in 1948–49, to study the problems of the introduced wapiti and make recommendations. At the end of that year, his alma mater Pacific University honored him with the degree of doctor of science, citing him as "a man of the world terrestrial, authority on its animal life, interpreter of nature's art, student of her design, exponent of the wilderness in terms of the human spirit!"

This quotation expresses well the various forces that operated in Olaus's character. His boyhood experience had developed in him the habit of never being idle, of constantly having projects under way, but still taking time for fun. Self-reliance, dependability, perseverance, never giving up in the face of difficulties—these qualities became part of him, together with an avid curiosity about every aspect of life.

The Murie children were taught to be dependable and resourceful in the out-of-doors, for their father believed that all children need woods, waters, and wild creatures. When very young they learned how to camp out, put up scientific specimens, and band birds, as well as how to cut wood, spade, rake, and plant a garden. But there were always playtimes, too, full of sheer joy, mimicry, and foolishness, for Olaus also believed that the out-of-doors lost its real purpose if it were not a world of joy.

Wherever Olaus traveled, children and young people were drawn to him. On his early expeditions into the then comparatively unexplored wilderness of Hudson Bay and Labrador, Indian and Eskimo children hovered around him, watching him as he prepared bird or mouse specimens, or made drawings of birds and animals they knew. He was a child with children and loved to play their games and to dance. When talking with them, he might suddenly break into a jig, all of them laughing together. Mardy Murie says that one of her most precious possessions is a snapshot of Olaus dancing with a group of Eskimos on Nunivak Island. Young people who knew Olaus seemed to sense his inner happiness in what he was doing, his innate faith in life and goodness, and his abiding belief in the young.

When the elk study was going on in Jackson Hole, he always had one or two boys in camp every summer to take part in the work. There was no formal teaching, for they were co-adventurers with him; but he answered their questions, and there was time for fun. As the years went by, there were young assistants on every expedition: to the Aleutians in 1936 and 1937; to New Zealand during the fiordlands expedition; and finally on the two expeditions to the Brooks Range in 1956 and 1961.

During his years of living in Jackson Hole and carrying on the work of The Wilderness Society, many young scientists and students came to see Olaus. When they asked his advice on education and training, he always replied: "Get a broad liberal education first, then decide what your specialty should be!" He would further advise them not to take themselves too seriously and to get out into the wilderness often enough to keep their perspective on life in general.

Olaus Murie received much recognition during his life: the Wildlife Society Award for the outstanding ecological publication (1951); the Aldo Leopold Memorial Medal (1952); the Cornelius Amory Pugsley Bronze Medal from the American Scenic and Historic Preservation Society (1954); the Audubon Medal from the National Audubon Society (1959); the Conservation Award of the American Forestry Association (1955); the Izaak Walton League Honor Roll in Conservation (1960); and the John Muir Award of the Sierra Club (1963).

But the event that brought him the greatest happiness was the executive order of Secretary of the Interior Fred Seaton in 1960 that set aside nine thousand square miles of northeastern Alaska as the Arctic National Wildlife Range. Olaus deeply loved this part of the Arctic and saw it as a great sanctuary for the innocent, free-roving wild things, a sanctuary that men—a very few at a time—could now quietly and gently share, but never alter.

This page intentionally left blank

PRONUNCIATION GUIDE
TO NATIVE WORDS

Note: All of the following are Eskimo words except those indicated by an asterisk, which are Indian. The names of persons, places, and ships below are not translated.

	Pronunciation		*Pronunciation*
*Alatna**	À-lăt'-nà	*Koksoak*	Kōk'-sō-ahk
*Allakaket**	Ăllà-kăk'-et	*Kusilvak*	Kōō'-sil-văk
Askinuk	Ăs'-kĭn-ŭk'	*Mose Odjik*	Mōz'-ō-jeek'
*Denali**	Děn-ah'-lee	*Patuktok*	Pa-tŏŏk'-tok
Inenew	In'-neh-new	*Pootuok*	Pōō '-tu-ok
Kaniapiskau	Kan-iă'-pĭs-kaủ	*Wetunnok*	Wee-tŭn'-ŭck

Akpaines!...Ahk-pī'-nès
"Oh, dear," or "Oh, horrors!"

Aksunai!...Ahk-shŭ-nī'
"Farewell!"

amisoot...ahm-i-soot'
"many"

angiok...ahng'-i-awk
"much, big"

imak...ē-mahk'
"like this"

Kahtsik ahput peetehungetok...................Kaht-sik ahpŭt peete-hung'e-tŏ
   tekkolaukreet?   tĕkko-lauk'-reet?
"How old are you?"

(Reply) Ahwettinget...................................Ahwĕt-ting'-ĕt
   pingashurroktut-lo   pingà-shŭr-rŏk'-tŭt-lo
"Twenty-six."

Kopinua angoraka...................................Ko-pin-u'-a ahn'-go-ra-ka
"Little-bird white man"

metiuk...mēē'-tee-ŭk
"eider"

Nekugmik!...Neh'-kug-mik
"Thanks!"

oogrook ....ōōg'-rŏŏk
"bearded seal"

shogenosh ....shah'-gė-nŏsh
"white man"

Shunowna? ....Shŭ-now'-na?
"What is the name of that?"

Siko audlat! ....Sēē'-kō owd'-laht
"The ice is going!"

toolualuk ....tōō-lōō-ah'-lŏŏk
"raven"

tsavili ....tsah-vĭ-lee'
"old harpoon points"

GLOSSARY

ARCTIC ZONE: the life zone found on the treeless plains north of timberline in the northern hemisphere.

AURORA BOREALIS ("northern lights"): the luminous sky display caused by minute particles from the sun coming into contact with the magnetic field of the earth.

AVIFAUNA: the birds typically found in a specific area or time period.

CAPSTAN: a machine used to raise heavy weights (such as anchors) by winding a cable around a drum that is rotated by hand, steam, or electric power.

CLUTCH: a group of newborn birds; a nest of eggs.

DENALI **("The Highest One"):** the Indian name for Mount McKinley, the highest peak in North America.

DUNNAGE: padding—such as mats or small pieces of wood—used to cushion a transported article; baggage or personal belongings.

FLAGELLATE: a diminutive, unicellular organism having a long, whiplike body.

FJORD: a narrow, often deep, inlet of the sea between sheer slopes or cliffs.

GEE POLE: a pole located at the front of a dogsled that is used to steer the vehicle.

GLARE ICE: ice with an untracked, slippery-smooth surface.

HUMMOCK: a slight rise in land; a rounded knoll; a mound of ice that has been broken by the force of pressure.

INFUSORIA: any of numerous microscopic bodies, especially those of the phylum Protozoa and the order Rotifera, found in stagnant water.

LICHEN: plants composed of an alga and a fungus growing in a mutually supportive association on rock and bark. A species of lichen called reindeer moss provides nourishment for caribou.

LIFE ZONE: an environment characterized by distinct physical conditions and inhabited by communities of particular types of organisms.

MUSKEG: a swamp, often thickly covered with a tangle of sphagnum moss, tussock, and other water plants that make it a difficult area to cross.

OVERFLOW ICE: water forced upward by pressure to break through and overflow an ice surface, where it freezes. This process may be repeated until the overflow ice is an average of three or four feet thick.

PAC: a rubber-bottomed, waterproof, leather-laced shoe, similar to a moccasin, that is worn in the wet tundra regions of the North.

PERMAFROST: permanently frozen ground, whose elements are cemented together by ice, found sporadically at various depths below the surface in Arctic regions. Permafrost gives off enough surface moisture, however, to support a flourishing, varied flora in Arctic Alaska.

PLEISTOCENE EPOCH: the Great Ice Age, an interval of approximately one million years, during which early man appeared and continental glaciers moved over North America. The pressure of ice sheets on mountains during this period formed the present river valleys and coastlines.

PORTAGE: haulover; the carrying of canoes and gear overland to avoid a rapids or to reach one body of water from another.

RIME: a crust of granular ice tufts; hoarfrost.

STEELYARD: lever scales; a portable device that measures weight by the movement of a counterpoise along a long arm until it balances and equals the weight of an object suspended from the shorter arm of the lever.

TAIGA: moist, subarctic forest covered with fir and spruce.

TUNDRA: the treeless, often soggy plain between the ice cap and the timberline of Arctic regions, characterized by black topsoil and a permanently frozen subsoil that supports a heavy growth of moss, stunted shrub, and lichen.

TUSSOCK: a tuft of grass; a hillock of more solid ground in a bog.

WITHES: flexible willow branches used by the early Indians in Alaska in putting up caribou snare fences. The branches were twisted around the rails and held them in place.

INDEX